CASES IN AUDITING

Second edition

JOSEPHINE MALTBY
Sheffield University Management School

P·C·P
Paul Chapman
Publishing L

Josephine Maltby is a chartered accountant. She worked for Ernst & Young as a senior audit manager before taking up her present post as a lecturer in accounting at Sheffield University Management School.

Copyright © 1996 Josephine Maltby

Paul Chapman Publishing Ltd
144 Liverpool Road
London
N1 1LA

British Library Cataloguing in Publication Data

Maltby, Josephine
  Cases in auditing – 2nd ed.
  1. Auditing 2. Auditing – Case Studies 3. Auditing – Problems,
  exercises, etc.
  I. Title
  657.4.'5

ISBN 1 85396 312 7

Typeset by Dorwyn Ltd, Rowlands Castle, Hampshire
Printed and bound in Great Britain

A B C D E F G H 9 8 7 6

Contents

Acknowledgements

I should like to thank the following for their assistance with this book:

Leigh Holland of De Montfort University who contributed the Softdream Limited case.

David Stephens of Ernst & Young and David Starr of Grant Thornton, who kindly designed and provided me with material which I have used in the following cases:
Ernst & Young: Elliott Transmitters plc; Esparto Limited.
Grant Thornton: Holiday Holdings Limited.

R. A. Rickson of Extel Financial, 37–45 Paul Street, London EC2A 4PB for permission to use material from a card compiled by Extel Financial in the case of the Banbury Group plc.

Mike Hayes and Bill Speirs for advice in compiling the Brighter Alloys Limited case.

The UK Competent Body for the EC Eco-Management and Audit Scheme for permission to use quotations from their publication *An Introductory Guide for Industry*.

Chris Humphrey and Dave Owen of Sheffield University Management School for their advice and comments.

Valerie Patrick for her assistance in preparing the manuscript of this book.

Marianne Lagrange of Paul Chapman Publishing for her advice, enthusiasm and encouragement.

Series Editor's Preface

Since the publication of the first edition of Josephine Maltby's *Cases in Auditing* in 1991 there have been a number of significant developments in both the practice of auditing and the regulatory framework within which it operates. As auditors try to improve both the quality and efficiency of their audit work there is an increasing emphasis on a risk-based approach to auditing and a more extensive use of information technology in the audit process. Similarly, auditors are concerned that they should be giving added value to their clients, for example by extending the range and scope of issues covered in management letters. At the same time, the environment in which auditors fulfil their statutory responsibilities is more heavily regulated and more litigious. Professional accountancy bodies are required to ensure that they have proper procedures for monitoring the competence of auditors, and the standards and guidelines published by the Auditing Practices Board are intended to enhance the quality of the work carried out by auditors.

It is not surprising, therefore, that Josephine Maltby has now written a second edition of *Cases in Auditing* which reflects many of these changes. The second edition contains seven new cases, covering such important topics as auditor liability, corporate governance, risk-based auditing and independence. The addition of these new cases reflects the fact that the modern, up-to-date, auditor must not only be technically competent but must also recognize the changing nature of auditing and the audit environment. Furthermore, in most of these cases the auditor is placed in a confrontational position with the client where the use of tact and compromise is a necessity. These cases, therefore, will provide a new challenge for students, requiring them to use their judgement and negotiating skills as well as creativity and imagination in their search for solutions to these real world problems.

During the last five years *Cases in Auditing* has been selected by scores of lecturers as one of the principal texts in their auditing courses. Consequently, all the cases have been thoroughly tested in the classroom and the author has received valuable feedback from users which has been very helpful in putting together the second edition. It is a mark of the success of the first edition that just one of the original cases has been removed and only two others have needed to be revised. In the original Series Editor's Preface in 1991 I wrote that *Cases in Auditing* "will soon become the standard by which other auditing case study books are judged". Since then, there have been no other auditing case study books which have even approached that standard. Now there is one which has surpassed it; the second edition of *Cases in Auditing*!

Michael Sherer
University of Essex

Introduction

The aim of this book is to act as a supplement, and perhaps sometimes a corrective, to the auditing textbooks in current use in undergraduate and professional courses. Such texts give a thorough account of the requirements of the auditing standards and guidelines and of the way in which these should be implemented in different audit areas. The student is given a clear and comprehensive overview of the auditing process, from planning via testing to the final audit opinion, together with detailed suggestions for the kind of tests which are appropriate to different audit areas.

The disadvantage of studying auditing through these books is that though they outline the procedures to be followed, they give the student little idea of what happens when these procedures have to be applied to a real situation. Auditing appears to be the more or less mechanical performance of a number of predetermined steps – a duller, but also a much less problematical activity than it actually is.

Cases in Auditing has been written with the intention of introducing students to the problems that arise in applying auditing standards and guidelines in practice. The case study format was adopted because, in the words of Easton (1982, p. 5), 'The case method is primarily a vehicle for developing skills'. Easton identifies six major skills which can be developed by the case method: analytical, application, creative, communication, social and self-analysis skills. Two of these skills – analysis and application – are particularly relevant to the teaching of auditing. This may be illustrated by considering the role of evidence in auditing. Sherer and Kent (1983, pp. 51–2) stress the fundamental importance of evidence to the audit process, but also state clearly the problems that face the auditor in identifying and evaluating audit evidence:

> the concept of evidence in auditing is far less well defined than it is in law. In a court of law experts represent each side and have a duty to make a case by presenting all the evidence which they can: to regulate the procedure there are well defined rules concerning admissibility, and the final decision as to relevance and validity is made by the judge and jury.
>
> This is not the case with respect to auditing. There are no rules of admissibility. The auditor has access to an enormous amount of existing evidence in the form of the company's books and records and can obtain more from the company's officials, his *[sic]* own efforts and third parties. He must recognize that which is not relevant and discard it; he must recognize that which is relevant and accord it its due weight in his considerations.

Cases in Auditing attempts to introduce students to the problems presented by what Hatherley (1980) calls the audit evidence process, and thereby to develop their analytical skills. Each case contains data in various forms,

including systems descriptions, financial statements and extracts from accounting records, notes of meetings and discussions and the results of audit
tests. The student is required to analyse the data in order to:

1. identify potential problem areas;
2. identify those parts of the data which constitute relevant audit evidence;
3. determine how complete and reliable that evidence is.

Not all the information contained in the case will be relevant to the problem;
sometimes the conclusions drawn from it by the auditor will be invalid. The
student will need to use judgement to assess the evidence available and determine how it might be supplemented by other audit work.

Application skills are closely linked to analytical ones. Analysis is needed to
identify the problem and the relevant evidence; the next step is for the auditor
to determine which audit tests are appropriate in the circumstances. This is
not simply a matter of enumerating all the tests possible on a given audit area.
Certain tests may not be possible for a number of reasons. A client's system
may be defective or non-existent, so that controls are not there to be tested.
Time pressures may make other types of testing impossible – for instance, if
the audit deadline comes very close to the year-end. Fee pressures may have
an impact on the work done; the auditor will have to ensure that only the most
cost-effective tests are performed, so that there is inevitably some trade-off
between time taken and degree of assurance obtained.

Analysis and application combine in devising an audit approach that is
tailor-made to a specific situation. The student has to determine both what
audit work is necessary and what is possible, given the constraints that exist.

HOW TO USE THIS BOOK

The cases in this book are intended to cover all stages in the audit, from the
inception of a new engagement to the clearance of outstanding matters. They
are of varying length and difficulty, but there is no ascending order of
complexity.

The cases can be tackled either by a student working alone or by groups of
students preparing the work in advance for a class discussion. Most cases are
too long to be dealt with from scratch in an hour's tutorial. The solution notes
on disk contain the following information.

1. A brief summary of the material the case is intended to cover: this will not
   be exhaustive, in that it is impossible to test one aspect of the audit process
   completely in isolation. For instance, a case dealing with the audit of stocks
   will draw upon such areas as audit planning, systems testing and substantive testing in general.
2. Suggested readings: these are based principally on auditing standards and
   guidelines, occasionally supplemented with references to other sources in
   areas where official guidance does not exist.

Case 1
Alhambra Bingo Clubs

BACKGROUND

Gwynn & Co. is a small firm of chartered accountants in Cardiff. The audit partner has been asked to make a proposal to Alhambra Bingo Clubs (ABC), a Cardiff-based company, which wants to change from its present auditors.

PEOPLE INVOLVED

Gwynn & Co.
Ron Dare (RD): Senior Partner
Louise Gordon (LG): Audit Partner
Tim West (TW): Audit Senior

Alhambra Bingo Clubs
Simon Kramer (SK): Financial Director
Peter Foley (PF): Accountant

DOCUMENTS

1.1 Gwynn & Co. – Memorandum

From   RD
To   LG   *7 January 19X8*

Louise
I was introduced to Simon Kramer at the golf club on Saturday. He is a director of Alhambra Bingo Clubs. His father, Jack, is the MD and gradually retiring from active involvement with the company. I get the impression that Howells, who are ABC's present auditors, were Jack's choice and Simon fancies a change to somebody a bit more dynamic. They haven't fallen out with Howells, but I gather that Simon wants advice about computerizing ABC's system, which Howells can't provide.

Simon has asked us to make a proposal. Would you like to go and see him to glean a bit of information about the company?

Ron

1.2   Gwynn & Co. – Memorandum

From   LG
To   TW   *9 January 19X8*

Tim

I've made an appointment to see the financial director of ABC on 13 Jan. Will you come along too, please, and interview the financial accountant, Peter Foley? We need to assemble as much information as possible about ABC's business and systems so that we can plan the audit in outline.

LG

1.3   Extract from note of a meeting with Simon Kramer at ABC's offices on 13 January 19X8

I asked SK to give me a potted history of ABC. He explained that it was formed in the 1920s and had initially owned a chain of cinemas in South Wales. Jack began converting them to bingo halls in the 1960s and also acquired a couple of clubs from other operators. There are now 15 ABC clubs, all in Wales and the West of England.

Simon is planning a major acquisition. A company in Bristol has contacted ABC to ask whether they are interested in acquiring 6 clubs in that area which will be put on the market in July this year. ABC will need a bank loan of about £250k to finance the purchase and the bank will want to see up-to-date audited accounts to support the application. SK stressed that the audit must therefore be completed by 1 July at the latest. (This may give us problems, as ABC's year-end is 31 May and we are normally fairly busy in June. I didn't mention this to Simon, though.)

Simon isn't involved in day-to-day accounting. He leaves that to Peter Foley, who is unqualified but very experienced and has been with ABC for 7 years. I got the impression that the accounting staff are under a lot of pressure. As the number of clubs has increased, Peter and his staff have become increasingly snowed under with work. The club managers 'aren't recruited on their book-keeping ability' (according to SK) and they can be quite slapdash about making returns. Peter spends a lot of time chasing them for overdue informa-tion. A computer would definitely help, but nobody in the company has much idea of what to buy. Simon confirmed that, if we are appointed, he would like us to advise them about systems improvements in general and computerization in particular.

He also mentioned that Howells gave ABC assistance in preparing the statutory accounts, and were responsible for the company's tax computation. He would like us to take over these functions ...

We agreed that I would send him a proposal, setting out the likely level of our fees and the service we can offer.

1.4 ABC – Organization chart

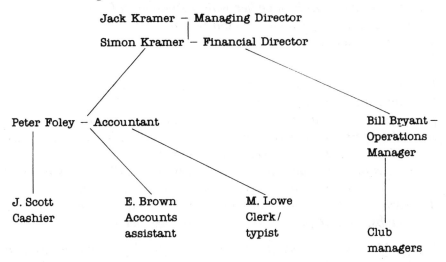

1.5 ABC Ltd – Brief systems notes

Prepared by TW 13.1.X8

There are 3 main activities at the clubs – bingo games, gaming (i.e. 'fruit') machines and café sales.

BINGO *Clubs have 2 sessions daily – afternoon and evening. Members pay an admission fee and then so much per bingo card. Most of the card price (less gaming duty) is paid out again as prize money.*

Cards issued are sequentially numbered and all numbers have to be accounted for by club management. This is a control to ensure that all proceeds from card sales are received by the company.

ABC is required to keep detailed records of games played for gaming duty purposes. Club managers make a weekly return to head office of cards sold and cash taken.

GAMING MACHINES *ABC rents all its gaming machines from Havago Ltd. A Havago collector visits each club once a week, unlocks and empties each machine and hands over the takings to the club manager, less £20 rent. The collector fills in a return showing the amount of the takings and sends a copy to ABC's head office (HO).*

CAFÉ SALES   *A till is installed in each café. Managers send till rolls to HO each week, together with a summary of takings.*

HO accounts staff collate the club returns, review them for possible errors and discrepancies and enter the weekly totals in the nominal ledger.

BANK & CASH ACCOUNTS   *Managers are responsible for banking cash. They send the paying-in slips to HO. Each club has a petty cash float of a set amount − £100 to £250, depending on club size. Managers record payments in a club petty cash book. They are allowed to use cash from takings to reimburse the float.*

There is one bank account, controlled by HO. All cheques must be signed by a director. Club managers have no access to the bank account. The cashier writes up the cash book, using the paying-in data received from clubs, and prepares a monthly bank reconciliation.

PURCHASES   *Apart from petty cash purchases, all goods and services are paid for by HO. Managers approve purchase invoices by signing them and then send them to HO for payment. HO enters them in the purchase ledger and sends cheques directly to suppliers.*

Apparently there was a problem last year-end as some managers were late in sending in purchase invoices relating to purchases before the year-end and creditors were understated as a result.

FIXED ASSETS   *The main tangible ones are the freeholds of 4 clubs (Swansea, Swindon, Hereford and Cardiff; the other clubs are leasehold) and the newly installed fixtures and fittings at Swansea and Hereford. Equipment in the other clubs is largely fully depreciated.*

STOCK   *This is mainly canteen supplies and stationery − bingo cards and tickets. Club managers do a count every month.*

GENERAL   *PF and his staff seem efficient but are clearly under pressure in dealing with all the returns they get from clubs.*

PF commented that he expects to see a lot of the auditors again this year. Apparently Howells normally spend several weeks checking from the club returns to the nominal ledger. They also counted cash and took stock at all the clubs during the week after the year-end.

1.6 ABC Ltd – Summarized accounts for the year ended 31.5.X7

	£m
Turnover	2.4
Expenses:	
Wages	0.9
Clubs (rent, rates, light & heat etc.)	0.5
Depreciation	0.1
HO (salaries, legal & professional etc.)	0.3
	—
Profit before tax	0.6
Taxation	0.2

Retained profit	0.4

Fixed assets	2.0
	—
Stock	0.1
Bank	0.2
Cash	0.2

	0.5

Creditors	0.6
Net assets	1.9
	—
Share capital	1.0
Retained profits	0.9
	1.9
	—

1.7 Summary of branch results for the year ended 31.5.X7

(All £000)

BRANCH		Turnover	Club expenses	Cash at year-end	Stock at year-end
1	Abergavenny	165	50	25	9
2	Cardiff	360	60	30	13
3	Cheltenham	180	35	11	10
4	Fishguard	55	12	5	1
5	Hereford	115	29	10	1
6	Llanelli	180	60	15	5
7	Monmouth	100	24	7	6
8	Neath	85	13	8	7
9	Newport	170	40	15	12
10	Porthcawl	75	16	5	2
11	Port Talbot	260	46	17	3
12	Swansea	255	40	20	11
13	Swindon	130	22	10	4
14	Tenby	95	23	8	10
15	Weston	175	30	14	6
		2400	500	200	100

QUESTIONS FOR DISCUSSION

1. Assume that ABC's directors accept Gwynn & Co.'s proposal. What steps must Gwynn & Co. now take? Suggest the contents of any letters they will need to write.
2. Prepare a plan for the 19X8 audit. It should cover:
   (a) the timing of the audit;
   (b) locations to be visited;
   (c) nature of audit tests to be performed;
   (d) any possible problem areas.

Relevant reading

SAS 100: *Objective and general principles governing an audit of financial statements*
(APC Auditing Standard 101: *The auditor's operational standard*)
SAS 140: *Engagement letters*
(APC Auditing Guideline 406: *Engagement letters*)

Case 2
Elliott Transmitters plc

BACKGROUND

Elliott Transmitters (ET) imports and sells special telephone equipment such as portable telephones and car phones and also walkie-talkies. Its customers include chain stores, mail order companies and wholesalers. ET's year-end is 31 December. It is early July and the audit team is carrying out the interim audit for the 1989 year-end. The senior in charge of the interim audit has prepared an audit planning memorandum, which sets out the salient features of ET's business and performance in the past twelve months.

DOCUMENTS

2.1 Extract from audit planning memorandum

SALES AND DEBTORS

Latest figures (unaudited)

	6 months to 30.6.89 £000	Year ended 31.12.88 £000
Gross sales	1,677	3,518
	------	------
Trade debtors	507	467
Doubtful debt provision	(5)	(5)
	------	------
	502	462
	------	------

ET has about 275 customers. The average debt collection period is 7 weeks. In the past, ET has had very few bad debts; the total write-off for the year ended 31 December 1988 was less than £2,000. The company attributes this to the intensive credit investigations to which it subjects prospective customers. Customers must have their creditworthiness checked by a commercial agency before they are allowed credit. They are then assigned a credit limit; ET refuses to supply goods if this would take them over the limit. Each month, the computer produces an aged list of ledger balances. All customers who are overdue (i.e. with balances over 30 days old) are sent a reminder letter.

7

STOCKS

ET carries about 45 different lines in stock. All movements of stock are shown on a monthly stock ledger print-out produced by the computer. The company has a physical count of major stock lines monthly and all stock at the year-end. Stocks at 30.6.89 were £554k (31.12.88 £494k). There appear to have been some large stock losses which came to light during the June stocktake. These are still being investigated.

ACCOUNTING SYSTEM: CHANGES SINCE LAST YEAR

The company has recently introduced a small computer into the sales system. Despatch notes are produced manually and input to the computer. It then produces invoices, posts them to the books of account and prints summaries and reports at the end of the month.

2.2 Detailed analytical review (extracts)

£000	TURNOVER 1989	
	BUDGET	*ACTUAL*
Jan	300	276
Feb	340	325
Mar	330	280
Apr	350	267
May	310	265
Jun	300	264
	1,930	1,677

%	GROSS MARGIN	
Jan	25	24
Feb	26	27
Mar	24	25
Apr	25	23
May	26	31
Jun	25	19

I discussed the fluctuations in gross margin with the assistant accountant, Sally Green. She stated that the sharp drop in margin in June is thought to be possibly the result of stock losses. The company is currently investigating the position.

2.3 Organization chart

The personnel involved in the sales system are:

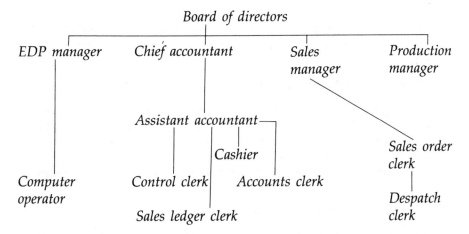

2.4 Transcript of an interview with sales manager

John Vaz (V), an audit trainee, interviewed Judith Andrews (A), the sales manager, as a preliminary to documenting the sales system. The conversation went as follows:

V   I believe all the sales orders are received and processed here: is that right?

A   Yes.

V   Good. Shall we start with the receipt of a customer's order? How do you receive these? Do they come in by post or telephone or fax?

A   Mostly on the customer's own order form. We sometimes get telephone orders, but then we insist they are confirmed in writing by the customer. Anyway, we immediately transfer the order on to our own sales order form and work out the value. Then we use the internal form to check whether the item is in stock. If it is, we mark the sales order form accordingly.

V   What then?

A   We make out an order confirmation for those items that we have in stock and note on the bottom of the confirmation the items which are either out of stock or not quickly obtainable. If none of the items ordered is in stock then I write a rejection letter giving the reason. I compare the customer order with our sales order and the confirmation. Then I sign the confirmation and send it off. We file the sales order with the original order.

V   How are they filed?

A   In customer account number order.

V   Where do you get the number from?

A   Oh, I forgot to mention that! Mary, the sales order clerk, puts it on the sales order when we have checked that the customer is within his credit limit.

V   When and how do you do that check?

A   I suppose that's the first thing we do, really. It's so automatic I forgot about it. As soon as we've priced the sales order, Mary examines the aged analysis of debtors in the accounts department. She looks at the current balance and compares it with the credit limit. If she sees that the customer has an account and is within his limit, she enters his account number on the order.

V   What if he doesn't already have an account?

A   We ask a credit rating agency to investigate his creditworthiness. If they write to say that his credit is good, I enter customer details, account number and credit limit on a sales ledger master file amendment form. Then I file the letter on the customer master file. I send the master file amendment form to data processing for input to the computer. If I didn't approve the account, we would send a rejection letter and file it with the copy letter and the rejected order. This would be alphabetically filed by customer name.

V   Is there any procedure for reviewing credit limits?

A   How do you mean?

V   I mean checking whether a customer should be given a lower level of credit, if his financial position worsened, for instance.

A   No, we don't do that.

V   Let's see now; you said an order confirmation was made out after you'd checked on stock availability. How many copies of the confirmation are there?

A   There are 4 copies in pre-numbered sets.

V   And what happens to them?

A   The top copy goes to the customer. We send the second copy to the despatch department who use it to select the goods and make up the order. The third copy goes to the sales ledger clerk and Mary files the fourth in alphabetical order by customer name.

V Do you check the price quoted by the customer on the original order?

A No. Our terms of sale are that goods will be invoiced at the price ruling on the date of delivery.

V Fine. I think that's told me what I need to know about the process for accepting orders. Thanks for your help.

2.5 Flowchart: procedure for making up and despatching orders

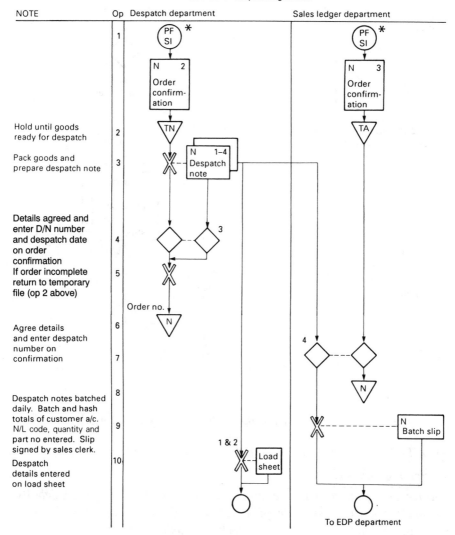

ELLIOTT TRANSMITTERS
Procedures for despatching orders

* Refers to an earlier part of the file which charted the process for taking orders

ELLIOT TRANSMITTERS
Procedures for despatching orders

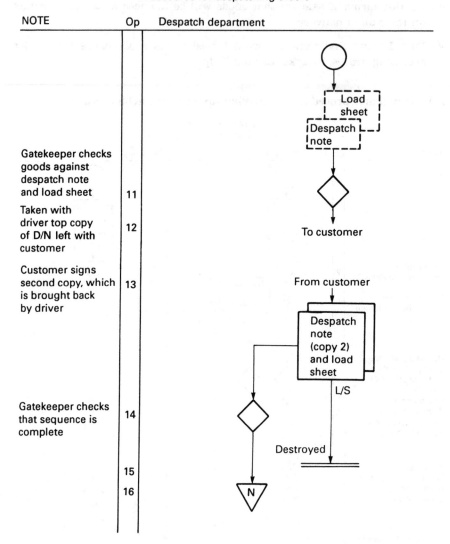

NOTE	Op	Despatch department

Gatekeeper checks goods against despatch note and load sheet — 11

Taken with driver top copy of D/N left with customer — 12

Customer signs second copy, which is brought back by driver — 13

Gatekeeper checks that sequence is complete — 14

15

16

[*The following is an extract from the audit team's system notes.*]

STOCK AVAILABILITY CHECK (*Flowchart ref. 5*)

1. STOCK AVAILABLE

On receipt of an order, the order details are checked for availability against the stock master file print-out and the order quantity deducted from the balance, to show the stock available (free stock). The sales order is marked with an 'A' to indicate availability.

2. STOCK UNAVAILABLE

The procedure is similar to that in 1 above. Items which are not available are marked 'R' (reorder) on the sales order and a letter is sent to the customer explaining that the goods are temporarily out of stock. A note is made on the order confirmation of the items not available.

2.6 Notes on the sales invoicing and sales ledger system

I discussed the sales invoicing and sales ledger system with the EDP manager and the assistant accountant. The system appears to operate as follows:

1. *Despatch notes are batched daily in the despatch department (see details in Document 2.5 above) and sent to EDP department. The data control clerk checks that the number of documents received agrees with the batch slip.*

2. *The clerk then enters individual despatch note details and batch totals into the mainframe computer. An edit program on the computer checks the batch total and the correctness of the account numbers used. (A check digit prevents invalid numbers from being accepted by the computer.) An error report is produced listing any input errors. These are then corrected by the control clerk and re-input and the error report is filed in date order.*

3. *The control clerk also inputs cash received sheets and journal adjustment sheets. These are prepared by the assistant accountant and are respectively a listing of cash received from customers and a listing of corrections to sales ledger accounts. Input of these is also checked via the error report.*

4. *After re-inputting as necessary, the clerk has produced a validated batch file. Every week this is run in the computer, together with the sales ledger master file, which lists customer details and balances, and the sales price master file. This run produces:*
   - *sales day book (weekly)*
   - *sales invoices (3 copies) (weekly)*
   - *statements for all customers (monthly)*
   - *an aged analysis of balances (monthly).*

The sales day book is compared with the totals of the despatch notes, cash received sheets and journals input to ensure that all have been completely entered. It is then filed in date order in the accounts department.

The sales invoices are returned to the sales dept., where they are matched with despatch notes filed there, to ensure that every invoice corresponds to a despatch note. The sales ledger clerk checks the accuracy of the casts and calculations of all invoices. One copy is then sent to the customer and the other 2 are filed, one copy in accounts dept. and one in the sales dept. with the despatch note.

One copy of the statement is sent to the customer. The other is filed in the accounts department.

The aged analysis of debtors shows, for each customer, the total balance outstanding and breaks it down into the amounts which are:
<30 days old
31–60 days old
61–90 days old
>90 days old.
The chief accountant reviews it every month and overdue items are followed up.

A sales ledger control account is maintained in the nominal ledger and is reconciled every month by the chief accountant to the list of balances on the aged analysis.

2.7   Extract from audit manager's review of the interim work

QUERY	REPLY
1. Is there any check to ensure that all despatch notes have resulted in an invoice, e.g. by a sequence check of despatch notes on file?	1. No, but they check from invoices to despatch notes.
2. Is there any check that the sales price master file is correct?	2. Yes. Every week, the sales dept. agree a print-out of the masterfile to a price list approved by the sales manager.
3. Is there any check that the aged analysis of debts is correct?	3. No.

2.8   Extract from audit programme, sales and debtors section

The following are key control objectives in ensuring that sales and debtors are correctly stated.
1. Customer orders require approval of credit and terms before acceptance.

2. Uncollectable amounts are promptly identified and provided for.
3. Goods despatched or services rendered are invoiced.
4. Invoices are for the correct amount.
5. Sales are recorded correctly as to account, amount and period.
6. Recorded invoices are for valid transactions.

QUESTIONS FOR DISCUSSION

Preliminary note: An important feature of any real-life sales system would be a system for ensuring that credits given to customers (for faulty goods, returns, etc.) are correctly authorized and recorded. For reasons of simplicity, the sales credit system has not been included in this case study.

1. Flowchart the system for taking and accepting orders.
2. For each of the control objectives stated in Document 2.8, identify what you consider to be the key controls or weaknesses in the system.
3. Based on your work in Question 2, suggest appropriate audit tests to ensure that the control objectives are met and that sales and debtors are correctly stated. Remember that your tests need not be exclusively systems tests: substantive testing and analytical review may also be required.

Relevant reading

SAS 300: *Accounting and internal control systems and audit risk assessments*
(APC Auditing Guideline 204: *Internal controls*)
APC Auditing Guideline 407: *Auditing in a computer environment*

Case 3
Softdream Limited

BACKGROUND

Luca and Co. are the auditors of Softdream Limited, which owns a frozen food warehouse and a chain of three retail outlets in the town of Glory. The warehouse supplies a wide range of frozen foods to the shops, who do not obtain supplies from anywhere else. Luca and Co. have been the auditors for several years, and carry out an interim (systems) audit shortly before the year-end (which is 31 March) and a final audit in about June each year.

DOCUMENTS

3.1   Extract from audit manager's notes

Softdream has had a computerized accounting system maintained by the accountant and run on a PC; wordprocessing is computerized but all other applications have been manually produced. However, the company has computerized all its operations as from 1 April. The company has installed a network system using point-of-sale technology at the retail shops. This system not only produces the customer till receipts but also updates the shops' stock systems. Customers can pay by cash, cheque, debit card or credit card. There are no account customers.

The network has been installed so that there are terminals in the office block sited next to the warehouse, in the goods inwards and loading bay of the warehouse, and in each of the shop manager's offices, as well as at the point of sale. The file server is located in the accountant's office in the office block. The software available on the network includes a standard accounting package (integrated purchase ledger, cash book, nominal ledger), a stock updating program, a wordprocessing program, an email system, a customer database, as well as electronic point of sale software.

The outline of the physical delivery to and from the warehouse is as follows:

Goods delivered to the warehouse from suppliers are checked at the goods inwards bay against the goods received note (GRN), the details of which are entered via the terminal by the supervisor to update stock. The GRN is passed to the office, where it will be matched with the purchase invoice before updating the purchase ledger.

Goods are delivered to the shops three times a week. The manager at each shop is responsible for ordering, by reviewing the stock as recorded on the individual shop system and by anticipating future demand. The order is received by the loading bay staff who physically compile the order and, via the terminal, book out the goods on individual shop accounts. Goods are invoiced to the shops at cost. Staff at both the warehouse and in the shops physically verify the quantities of a number of goods lines against computerized records and amend these as necessary. This takes place monthly.

3.2 File note by audit partner

Many aspects of the computerised system are similar to the old manual system, but the following differences may merit attention in this year's audit testing:

- Information held can be downloaded onto floppy disk (or hard copy) by the shop managers – for instance stock quantities at each shop may be held on disk.
- Terminals may be operated by inexperienced personnel.
- Aspects of security may be overlooked.
- Transfer of records onto the network took place without any parallel running of manual records.
- All programs related to accounting, wordprocessing, customer databases etc. could, in theory, be accessed by any member of staff with (authorized) access to the network.
- There may be a lack of audit trail.

QUESTIONS FOR DISCUSSION

1. Prepare the audit planning memorandum in respect of the audit of the network, outlining the areas of special concern and indicating the audit considerations.
2. What additional information will now be contained in the permanent file?
3. How can computer-assisted audit techniques help in the audit of Softdream Limited?

Case 4
Esparto Limited

BACKGROUND

Esparto Ltd (E) is a paper and cardboard manufacturing company whose year-end is 31 March 1989. The auditors are visiting the company early in January 1989 in order to plan their audit approach for the 1989 year-end. They have obtained copies of the 1989 management accounts and are comparing these with budgets and actual results for previous years in order to gain an insight into E's performance and to identify any areas which may pose problems at the year-end.

DOCUMENTS

4.1 Esparto Limited: Summarized management accounts — Esparto Limited management accounts: balance sheets

	Actual			Budget	Actual movement	
	12M 31.3.87	12M 31.3.88	9M 31.12.88	9M 31.12.88	9M 89/12M 88	
	£000	£000	£000	£000	£000	%
Fixed assets	940	1,156	1,200	1,205	44	3.81
Current assets						
Stocks	407	441	280	320	−161	−36.50
Debtors	415	454	474	477	20	4.40
Due from subsidiaries	30	–	30	50	30	100.00
Bank and cash	101	–	–	6	–	–
	953	895	784	853	−111	−12.40
Current liabilities						
Bank overdraft	–	29	30	–	1	3.45
Obligations under finance leases	222	230	207	210	−23	−10.00
Creditors	350	380	296	330	−84	−22.10
Taxation	102	82	84	86	2	2.44
Proposed dividends	20	30	–	30	−30	−100.00
	694	751	617	656	−134	−17.84
Net current assets	259	144	167	197	23	15.97
Total net assets	1,199	1,300	1,367	1,402	67	5.15

Financed by:

					Movement	
Share capital	500	500	500	500	–	0.00
Reserves	639	740	807	842	67	9.05
Revaluation reserves	60	60	60	60	–	0.00
Total capital and reserves	1,199	1,300	1,367	1,402	67	5.15

Esparto Limited management accounts: profit and loss accounts

	Actual			Budget		Movement	
	12M 31.3.87	12M 31.3.88	9M 31.12.88	9M 31.12.88	12M 31.3.89	Bud. 89/Act. 88	
	£000	£000	£000	£000	£000	£000	%
Sales	3,769	3,949	2,952	3,115	4,153	204	5.17
Less: Direct materials	1,409	1,539	1,204	1,160	1,547	8	0.52
Direct labour	400	428	332	335	446	18	4.20
	1,960	1,982	1,416	1,620	2,160	178	8.98
Overheads	723	770	615	625	833	63	8.18
Gross profit	1,237	1,212	801	995	1,327	115	9.49

	Actual 12M 31.3.87 £000	Actual 12M 31.3.88 £000	Actual 9M 31.12.88 £000	Budget 9M 31.12.88 £000	Budget 12M 31.3.89 £000	Movement Bud. 89/Act. 88 £000	%
Selling and admin expenses	624	563	348	472	629	66	11.72
General expenses	425	432	350	321	429	–3	–0.69
Profit before tax	188	217	103	202	269	52	23.96
Taxation	85	86	36	70	93	7	8.14
Profit after tax	103	131	67	132	176	45	34.35
Dividends	20	30	–	30	40	10	33.33
Retained profit	83	101	67	102	136	35	34.65

Esparto Limited management accounts: overheads and expenses

	Actual 12M 31.3.87 £000	Actual 12M 31.3.88 £000	Actual 9M 31.12.88 £000	Budget 9M 31.12.88 £000	Budget 12M 31.3.89 £000	Movement Bud. 89/Act. 88 £000	%
Overheads							
Indirect labour	85	89	72	72	96	7	7.87
Rent	360	380	299	300	400	20	5.26
Rates	50	60	51	55	73	13	21.67
Power and light	80	70	58	52	69	–1	–1.43
Maintenance	65	22	22	36	48	26	118.18
Depreciation	59	81	63	64	85	4	4.94
Consumables	24	20	16	14	19	–1	–5.00
Finance charges	–	48	34	32	43	–5	–10.42
Total	723	770	615	625	833	63	8.18

General expenses						
Salaries	275	290	228	224	299	9	3.10
Office rent and rates	50	65	51	50	67	2	3.08
Telephone	3	5	3	2	3	−2	−40.00
Insurance	12	15	12	10	13	−2	−13.33
Bad debt provision	4	2	–	2	3	1	50.00
Audit	10	12	9	8	11	−1	−8.33
Sundries	2	1	1	1	1	–	0.00
Legal	17	15	13	7	9	−6	−40.00
Management charges	32	20	18	12	16	−4	−20.00
Repairs and renewals	20	7	15	5	7	–	0.00
Total	425	432	350	321	429	−3	−0.69
Selling expenses						
Salaries	70	74	37	36	48	−26	−35.14
Commission	30	32	25	30	40	8	25.00
Advertising and marketing	254	165	72	186	248	83	50.30
Travel and entertainment	55	62	33	40	53	−9	−14.52
Carriage	215	230	181	180	240	10	4.35
Total	624	563	348	472	629	66	11.72

4.2 Extract from permanent audit file

The following schedule summarizes key ratios for Esparto Ltd since the year ended 31 March 1987.

	Actual			Budget
Key ratios	*12M*	*12M*	*9M*	*9M*
	31.3.87	*31.3.88*	*31.12.88*	*31.12.88*
Asset turnover	*3.14*	*3.04*	*2.16*	*2.22*
Debtors turnover	*9.08*	*8.70*	*6.23*	*6.53*
Average collection period	*40.19*	*41.96*	*43.99*	*41.96*
Average payment period	*90.67*	*90.12*	*67.36*	*77.95*
Current ratio	*1.37*	*1.19*	*1.27*	*1.30*
Quick ratio	*0.79*	*0.60*	*0.82*	*0.81*
ROCE	*0.16*	*0.17*	*0.08*	*0.14*

4.3 Extract from audit planning memorandum

GROUP STRUCTURE AND POLICY

Esparto Ltd is a wholly owned subsidiary of Parchment plc, a London-based multinational group. E's factory and offices are located in Worksop. E has a number of fellow subsidiaries in the UK. Parchment has adopted a policy in recent years of encouraging decentralization and local autonomy, so that decision-making is increasingly delegated to local management. Expenditure controlled at local level includes capital investment (up to a limit of £200,000) and all routine overheads, including marketing and advertising.

All dividends declared by Parchment subsidiaries are passed up to group headquarters. Parchment imposes a management charge on its subsidiaries to reflect their share of the services provided for them by the group, such as their use of group accounting and computing services. The management charge is determined centrally and is outside the control of individual subsidiaries. VAT is charged on the management charge.

ACTIVITIES

E produces different types of cardboard. It manufactures cardboard sheets, which it sells to fellow subsidiaries, and high quality corrugated cartons which it supplies to the whisky, chemical, electrical and food sectors. Its main raw material is paper, which it purchases directly from Sweden, paying for it in dollars. Different grades of paper are used, depending on the type of cardboard to be manufactured. It takes 6 weeks for E to receive an order from Sweden once it has been placed.

4.4　Extract from interview with David Weeks

Present: Jean Bailey (B), Audit Manager
　　　　　David Weeks (W), Managing Director of Esparto

B　Could you tell me what Esparto's sales targets are for the future?

W　Our aim is to achieve a steady 5% annual growth in sales while keeping gross contribution at about 52%.

B　And what action is the company taking to achieve this?

W　We're doing a number of things. Obviously, marketing is crucial. Our spending in that area has dropped over the last couple of years, but we intend to increase it significantly. We plan a big campaign in the relevant trade publications, and we shall be attending trade fairs and exhibitions in the UK and abroad. The quality of what we sell is very important too. We put a lot of stress on quality control, and we're steadily upgrading our fixed assets. Over the past 2 years, we've brought in new stitchers and glue units and made a number of improvements to the corrugating machine.

B　Is this a competitive market?

W　This is an extremely competitive market. There is substantial over-capacity at the moment, and the reaction in the industry is to cut prices and make special promotional offers. We have to push particularly hard for sales at the moment because we lost a major customer recently. It was Carton & Case, who were taken over by a competitor of ours, Containers plc. Naturally, Containers has got all their business, and we have to compensate for that ...

4.5　Extract from permanent audit file

BUDGET SYSTEM

E's budgeting system is largely dictated by the requirements of the Parchment group. The budgeting process begins in November each year, when divisional heads within E are required to submit outline budgets for their divisions. Particular stress is laid on the preparation of capital budgets for plant and equipment.

The management accountant, in conjunction with E's finance director, uses this information to prepare a budget for the company as a whole, which covers the 12 months from 1 April to 31 March. This company-wide budget is then discussed with the management team at Parchment, and simultaneously with divisional heads at E until a final budget has been agreed. This is then broken down again into divisional budgets and these are phased into monthly budgets.

Divisional results against budget are reported to, and monitored by, E's management accountant and financial director. E's overall results are reported to Parchment, together with an explanation of major variations from budget.

There is only limited scope for Parchment's subsidiaries to revise their budgets after 1 April each year. Revision would be permitted in case of a major upheaval, such as the closure or complete reorganization of a plant, but 'fine-tuning' the budget does not occur.

QUESTIONS FOR DISCUSSION

1. You are responsible for planning the audit of Esparto for the year ending 31 March 1988. Using the information the case study gives about the company, identify those areas which you consider to present potential audit risks.
2. Using the schedules summarizing management accounts, identify the main trends in the company's performance this year. What questions should the auditor ask in order to gain a fuller understanding of E's performance and prospects?

Relevant reading

SAS 410: *Analytical procedures*
(APC Auditing Guideline 417: *Analytical review*)

Case 5
The Enormous Electrical Company

BACKGROUND

The Enormous Electrical Company Ltd (EE) was formed in March 19X8 by the merger of two smaller companies. It retails household electrical appliances of all kinds through a chain of thirty shops which it owns all over the UK. These are supplied from three warehouses, in Bristol, Birmingham and Glasgow. EE's first financial statements are for the period ending 31 December 19X8. The newly appointed financial controller drafted the stocktaking instructions to be followed by the warehouse and shop managers. The warehouse instructions are given in Document 5.1. EE's auditors attended all the three warehouse stocktakes (and a sample of the counts at shops). The audit working papers for the Bristol warehouse are given in Document 5.2.

DOCUMENTS

5.1 The Enormous Electrical Co. Ltd − Internal memo

FROM James Wilson, Financial Controller   4 November 19X8
TO   Peter Drake, Bristol warehouse
      Frank Moore, Birmingham warehouse
      Bill Drew, Glasgow warehouse

STOCKTAKING INSTRUCTIONS

1. The company's financial year-end will be 31 December 19X8 and a full count is to be carried out of all stocks held in the warehouses at that date. Please read the following instructions carefully and ensure that they are adhered to. Contact me as soon as possible if you need any clarification or if you anticipate any problems.

2. PREPARATION
The warehouse is to be tidied thoroughly in the week before the stocktake. Packing cases should be stacked as closely as possible, to allow staff to move freely. The warehouse is to be divided into clearly defined areas. Each area will be assigned to one of the warehouse staff, who will be responsible for counting the stock contained in it. The warehouse manager will be responsible for circulating these instructions to staff, dealing with any queries and ensuring that final stocksheets are sent to HO. It is also the responsibility of managers to identify obsolete or damaged stock.

3. COUNTING PROCEDURES

A sample stocksheet is shown in Appendix A to this memo. A supply of photocopies of this sheet is to be taken, for issue to staff. Staff should return completed sheets promptly to the warehouse manager. Each item of stock (case, box, etc.) should be marked with chalk when it has been counted. After completing the count, the person responsible should inspect the area to ensure that there are no unmarked items. Goods will have to be removed from the warehouse during 30 and 31 December, as they must reach shops in time for our January sale. As far as possible, counters should complete counting in their areas before allowing the movement of goods.

4. FOLLOW-UP

When all rough stocksheets have been returned, managers should review them and enquire into the reasons for any unexpectedly high or low stock figures. When this has been done, the rough sheets should be transcribed on to final sheets by a member of the clerical staff, to ensure that they are legible. The final sheets should then be returned to HO. Managers should make a note of the first goods inward and goods outward note numbers raised on 1 January 19X9 and send this information to HO for cut-off purposes.

Thank you in advance for your co-operation.

James

APPENDIX A

SPECIMEN STOCK SHEET

LOCATION

NAME OF STOCKTAKER

STOCK CODE   QUANTITY   UNIT*

* Specify boxes, dozen, each, etc.

5.2 Notes on attendance at the Enormous Electrical Co.'s stocktake at Bristol on 31 December 19X8

I attended EE's stocktake at its warehouse on the Excelsior Industrial Estate between 9.30 a.m. and 5.30 p.m. on 31 December. During this time, I discussed the stocktaking procedures with the warehouse manager, Mr Drake, and toured the warehouse to observe the stocktake. The warehouse was tidy and the count appeared to be going on in an orderly fashion, with items being marked off as they were counted. I performed the following test counts:

(a) From stock sheets to physical stock:

STOCK CODE	NOTES	QTY PER SHEET	QTY COUNTED
AJ123		12	12
M3000	(1)	6	5+1
F234		19	19
AS19		100	100
EM236		63	63
BII32		231	231
DE470	(2)	85	50
SR288		12	12
EM670		11	11
FH678		76	76
AK427		100	100
Q345	(3)	54	45
M2500		23	23
DJ688	(4)	16	13
SDD358		9	9

(b) From physical stock to stocksheets

STOCK CODE	NOTES	QTY COUNTED	QTY PER SHEET
QWE112		37	37
F1000		68	68
ET667	(5)	130	120
WSC987	(6)	335	339
EM457		34	34
W2790		32	32
DJ3456		23	23
DE379		8	8
DJ4326	(6)	97	100

Q3098		35	35
DF4563		98	98
JUS333		12	12
SD4578	(6)	500	510
FR8748		97	97
ED5544		18	18

NOTES:

(1) *The difference on this line — Hotpoint washing machines — arose because I originally omitted the one damaged machine which had been moved to a separate part of the warehouse.*

(2) *35 of this item had been removed from the warehouse for distribution to shops between the time they were counted and the time I carried out my test.*

(3) *9 of this item had been removed for distribution before I could count them.*

(4) *Presumably the same reason for the difference as in (2) and (3) above.*

(5) *This difference arose because I mistakenly counted 10 of item EX661 as ET667.*

(6) *I was unable to discuss these differences with the storeman responsible, as he had finished for the day and gone home. They seem to have been simple mistakes. However, since the items involved are relatively low-value ones — electric kettles, blankets and toasters — and the numbers involved are so large, the error cannot be described as material and does not require further investigation.*

Conclusion: On the basis of the work done and the explanations I have received, I conclude that the stocktake has been correctly carried out and the stock quantities notified to HO are materially correct.

QUESTIONS FOR DISCUSSION

1. What controls are present in the stocktaking instructions issued to the warehouse managers? What controls have been omitted and what effect might this omission have on the results of the stocktake?

2. In your opinion, is there any other audit work which should have been carried out at this stocktake? What would it have achieved? Do you consider that the auditor has drawn the right conclusions from his findings?

Relevant reading

APC Auditing Guideline 405: *Attendance at stocktaking*

Case 6
Technical Wizardry Limited

BACKGROUND

Technical Wizardry Ltd (TW) was originally set up in 1937 as the Typewriter Wholesaling Co. Ltd. The change of name reflects its strategy of moving into a new market in response to the decline in demand for typewriters and the increasing use of word processors and microcomputers in business. TW continues to sell typewriters but has gradually moved into the computer market, beginning by selling computer printers and going on to develop two computers of its own: the T700 and T35.

TW's year-end is 31 December and this case takes place in mid-January 19X1, during the latter part of the 19X0 audit. TW's profit before tax for 19X0 is expected to be about £15,000 on a turnover of £3 million. The auditors have completed the systems work and stocktaking attendance, with satisfactory results, and are now considering what tests need to be performed on stock valuation. Extracts from their working papers are given below.

DOCUMENTS

6.1 TW Ltd: stock summary

	19X0 £000	19Y9 £000
Typewriters	30	75
Printers	175	100
Typewriter spares	95	120
Printer spares	100	80
T700 computers	500	450
T35 computers:		
completed	50	–
work in progress	150	–
TOTAL	1,100	825

NB the 19X0 figures are subject to audit.

6.2 Extract from stock systems notes

Typewriter, printer and spares stock records are held on a microcomputer. Each different stock item is defined by a unique numerical code. Details of receipts of goods from suppliers and despatches to customers are input daily. The system can hold records of stock at 3 different purchase prices – current price and the 2 previous prices. It is rare for prices to change more often than twice a year. A number of reports can be produced by the computer, including:

Report no.	Frequency	Contents
001	Weekly	Receipts into stores analysed by stock code no.
002	Weekly	Issues from stores analysed by stock code no.
003	On demand	Movements over past 6 months of any stock item
004	Monthly	Aged analysis of stock by stock code no. and in total
005	Monthly	Stock items without any movement during the month
006	On demand	Current purchase price and previous price(s) over past 6 months of any stock item

The records for the stocks of T700 and T35 computers are kept manually on cards. The cards show the following information for each stock movement:

Date of receipt or issue
Quantity received/issued
Serial no of TW's goods received note/despatch note
Balance in stock

6.3 004 report totals at 31 December 19X0

```
TOTALS OF 004 REPORTS AS AT 31.12.X0
TYPEWRITERS                                    £
TOTAL STOCK                                 30174
< 1 MONTH OLD                                9756
1-2 MONTHS OLD                              11234
2-3 MONTHS OLD                               8756
3-4 MONTHS OLD                                428
```

4−5 MONTHS OLD	NIL
5−6 MONTHS OLD	NIL
6−12 MONTHS OLD	NIL
> 12 MONTHS OLD	NIL
PRINTERS	
TOTAL	174876
< 1 MONTH OLD	65756
1−2 MONTHS OLD	87432
2−3 MONTHS OLD	18904
3−4 MONTHS OLD	2784
4−5 MONTHS OLD	NIL
5−6 MONTHS OLD	NIL
6−12 MONTHS OLD	NIL
>12 MONTHS OLD	NIL
TYPEWRITERSPARES	
TOTAL	95023
< 1 MONTH OLD	1500
1−2 MONTHS OLD	34211
2−3 MONTHS OLD	15678
3−4 MONTHS OLD	10877
4−5 MONTHS OLD	NIL
5−6 MONTHS OLD	4566
6−12 MONTHS OLD	18888
> 12 MONTHS OLD	9303
PRINTER SPARES	
TOTAL	99566
< 1 MONTH OLD	45557
1−2 MONTHS OLD	27644
2−3 MONTHS OLD	13428
3−4 MONTHS OLD	7685
4−5 MONTHS OLD	3344
5−6 MONTHS OLD	1908
6−12 MONTHS OLD	NIL
> 12 MONTHS OLD	NIL

6.4   File note on T700s

T700s are manufactured for TW in Ruritania by a subcontractor. TW imports them, carries out a quality control check in its warehouse and test centre near Heathrow and then repackages the computers. Because Ruritanian wage levels are low, this is much cheaper than making the

T700 here in the UK. TW had some quality problems in the early years of this arrangement, but standards have improved as the Ruritanians gained experience and installed effective inspection procedures of their own. Returns last year were less than 0.25% of sales.

TW pays for the computers in Ruritanian drachmas (RDR). The price throughout 19X0 has been 6,000 RDR. In previous years, TW has bought RDR forward in order to reduce its exposure to exchange movements, but this year, for the first time it has bought spot, as a result of the finance director's theory that the RDR was overvalued and likely to fall heavily against the £. The average rate for the last 4 months of 19X0 has been:

Sept.	6.0 RDR	= £1
Oct.	5.5 RDR	= £1
Nov.	6.5 RDR	= £1
Dec.	7.5 RDR	= £1

Costs of handling, quality control and repackaging at the Heathrow site are estimated at £19 per machine, and this is added to the purchase price in the stock valuation.

At 31 December TW has 500 T700s in stock, all bought from Ruritania in the last 4 months. It has valued them at average cost. The finance director has calculated an average exchange rate based on the 4 month-end rates: 6.375 RDR = £1.

6.5   Extract from TW's price list effective from 1 January 19X1

	Gross	VAT	Net
	£	£	£
T700	1,725	257	1,468
T35	3,450	514	2,936

(NB: Discounts are available on bulk orders of T35s, starting at 7.5% for orders of 6. Ask your TW rep for further details.)

6.6   Audit file note on T35s

The T35 is a laptop microcomputer aimed in particular at sales representatives and others who need a small, easily portable computer. TW introduced it just over a year ago. Until August this year, T35s were manufactured for TW in Utopia on the same basis as the T700 in Ruritania. TW gradually became dissatisfied with the quality of the imports and took the decision to start production in the UK. A small electronics company, Chips With Everything Ltd, was acquired as a

TW subsidiary in May and began full-scale production of the computer in August.

There have been numerous production problems in the UK, because of the inexperience of the workforce and defects in components supplied. As a result, none of the T35s made in the UK has been sold. The finished goods stock represents the last of the Utopian production, mostly bought in October 19X0 and valued at a purchase price of £2,500 each. (Imported T35s were paid for in £ sterling.)

The work in progress (WIP) is all UK production and can be analysed as:

	£000
25% complete	20
50% complete	70
Held back for rectification	60
	150

WIP has been valued on the basis of its stage of completion. Costs accrue evenly over the production process. Finished cost of the UK-produced computers is £2,850 each.

The computers requiring rectification were completed in November. Inspection revealed that they suffer from a major fault which will require the disk drive to be removed and replaced at an estimated additional cost of approx £250 each. Replacement work will be carried out in January 19X1.

QUESTIONS FOR DISCUSSION

1. What problem areas do you see with regard to the valuation of TW's stock?
2. Assuming that systems testing and stocktaking attendance have had satisfactory results, what audit tests should now be performed to ensure that the stock valuation is correct or to identify any possible misstatement?

Relevant reading

ICAEW Statements on Auditing and Reporting 902: *Stock-in-trade and work in progress*

Case 7
Warehousemasters Limited

BACKGROUND

Warehousemasters Ltd (W) specializes in the design, manufacture and installation of tailor-made storage equipment. Its products and services range from a few yards of shelving to the design and installation of major warehouses.

Until recently, all W's sales were in the UK, but in the financial year just ended it undertook a major export drive in an attempt to improve its declining sales. This was successful and it now has customers in the USA and Italy.

W's auditors have as usual performed an interim audit visit to the company in August 19X7. The company's year-end (30 September) falls in their busy season and they try to perform as many tests as possible at the interim stage to save time later on. Mike Small, the senior in charge of the audit, is reviewing the interim tests with the aim of deciding what work should be done at the final audit, which is scheduled to start on 10 October. Work must be completed and the audit report signed by 31 October.

DOCUMENTS

7.1 Warehousemasters Ltd: Extracts from permanent audit file; sales systems notes

SALES OF GOODS
On despatch of the goods from the warehouse a multi-part despatch note is raised:
Copy 1 goes with goods to customer
Copy 2 is retained in stores dept to update records of stock levels
Copy 3 is sent to sales invoicing dept, used as basis for invoice and then
    filed with a copy invoice.
Despatch notes are sequentially numbered. Every period-end a check is performed to ensure that all despatch note numbers are accounted for, and any missing ones are followed up.

SALES OF SERVICES (design, consultancy etc.)
The computerized time accounting system records the costs of staff time. This is used as a basis for invoicing and a copy of the relevant print-out is filed with the sales invoice. Contracts are given sequential job numbers, and a sequence check is made periodically to ensure all have been invoiced on completion.

SALES LEDGER

This is interfaced with the sales invoicing system so that as invoices are raised they are automatically posted to the ledger.

A print-out of the ledger is run every period-end giving details of every account.

The layout of an account is typically as follows:

0003456 BLOGGINS LTD (CREDIT LIMIT £4000)

	CR	DR
1.3.X7 OPENING BAL	2345.00	
11.3.X7 INV NO 2347	1267.00	
23.3.X7 CASH		345.00
23.3.X7 CREDIT NOTE NO 126		500.00
31.3.X7 CLOSING BAL		2767.00
	3612.00	3612.00

Each customer is sent a monthly statement which is a duplicate of the sales ledger account.

AGED DEBTORS LISTING

This is printed every month and shows the balance on each account broken down by the age of the unpaid invoices:

ACC NO	TOTAL £	CURRENT MONTH £	0–30 DAYS £	30–60 DAYS £	60–90 DAYS £	>90 DAYS £
0003456	2767	1267	NIL	790	310	400

CREDIT CONTROL

New customers are required to produce 2 references — from a bank and a current supplier — before they are allowed credit. The amount allowed is decided by the credit controller.

The controller reviews the monthly aged listing and telephones customers whose balances include items more than 60 days old.

After items are > 90 days old, a reminder letter is sent, with a sterner letter 14 days later. 3 weeks thereafter, a late payer will receive a solicitor's letter and may eventually be sued.

7.2   Extracts from interim audit working papers (sales section)

Test 1

OBJECTIVE
To ensure that all invoices
(a) represent despatches of goods/provision of services;
(b) are arithmetically correct.

WORK DONE
Selected a representative sample of 25 invoices for goods and 25 for services.
(a) Traced details of goods via copy despatch notes to stock issue records, and traced services details to time sheet summary record maintained by Design and Consultancy Department.
(b) Checked additions and calculations on each invoice.
See attached for details. [NB: Not included in case study.]

RESULTS
No errors were found.

CONCLUSION
All invoices relate to provision of goods/services and are arithmetically correct.

Test 2

OBJECTIVE
To ensure that all invoices are correctly posted to the sales ledger.

WORK DONE
Selected a representative sample of 30 sales invoices and ensured that they had been posted to the correct customer's sales ledger account in the correct period.
   See attached for details. [NB: Not included in case study.]

RESULTS
No errors were found.

CONCLUSION
Invoices are correctly posted to the sales ledger.

Test 3

OBJECTIVE
To ensure that payments received from debtors are posted correctly to the sales ledger.

WORK DONE

Selected from the cash book a representative sample of 30 cheques received from debtors. Ensured that each had been
(a) posted to the correct debtor's account;
(b) matched to the invoices to which it related.
See attached for results. [NB: Not included in case study.]

RESULTS

All cheque receipts were correctly posted except:

DATE REC'D	CUSTOMER	£
15.5.X7	S. Spriggs	1,000
11.6.X7	Wareco Ltd	600

The amount from Spriggs arrived without a remittance advice so that it was not possible to establish what invoices it related to. Wareco is in financial difficulties and has agreed to pay off its balance in monthly instalments of £600. In both cases, the sales ledger clerk followed W's policy of applying unallocated amounts to the oldest balance first.

CONCLUSION

It appears that receipts are correctly posted to the sales ledger in accordance with W's policy.

Test 4

OBJECTIVE

To ensure that credit is given only to approved customers and that credit limits are not exceeded.

WORK DONE

(a) For a sample of 25 new accounts opened this year checked that 2 references had been taken up and that the credit controller had approved the level of credit given.
(b) For a sample of 25 accounts, compared credit limit with balance currently outstanding.
See attached for details. [NB: Not included in case study.]

RESULTS

(a) No references had been taken up for:
Frank Brewer Ltd. Apparently, this customer had placed an urgent large order for shelving which would have been lost if W had insisted on references before proceeding. References were subsequently received and proved satisfactory.
Megacorp Inc. This US customer was recommended by a close friend of the MD.

<u>Contadini.</u> *An Italian customer. No further explanation could be given.*

<u>Tevere.</u> *As for Contadini. Both these cos have fairly small balances.*

Otherwise, all customers selected had provided references before being given credit.

(b) On review of the sales ledger it appeared that about 40% of accounts balances exceeded the stated credit limit, so it was decided to abandon this test and discuss the situation with the credit controller. He explained that many credit limits were set years ago and have not subsequently been subjected to a formal review. W would lose customers if it held them to unrealistically low levels of credit, but he has not got the time or resources to carry out a full-scale review of old limits. He copes with this by sanctioning breaches of the limit where he is satisfied that customers are a good risk.

CONCLUSION

It appears that the company's stated policy on credit limits is not being adhered to.

Test 5

OBJECTIVE

To ensure that debtors exist and are correctly stated.

WORK DONE

Selected a sample of 25 sales ledger balances by choosing the one with the highest value for each letter of the alphabet. These represented 32% of the total sales ledger balance of £604,632 at 31 August. Wrote to the customer requesting confirmation. See attached sample letter and list of balances.

RESULTS

To be written up when replies are received.

SAMPLE DEBTORS CIRCULARIZATION LETTER

Dear Sir/Madam

According to our records, your balance with us at 31 August 19X7 was £----
due to us.

Our auditors, Thomas, Gordon & Co., wish to confirm this balance as part of their audit of our financial statements for the year ended 30 September 19X7. Would you please complete and sign the tear-off slip at the bottom of this letter and return it to our auditors in the enclosed envelope. If you disagree with the balance, please note on the slip the balance according to your records.

Thank you for your assistance.

Yours faithfully

J. BANKS
Financial accountant

I agree/disagree with the balance of £--- shown above as due from me at 31 August 19X7.

Signed ------------------
Position in company

DEBTORS CIRCULARIZED

NAME	£
1 Archer Ltd	11,234
2 Bowers Partnership	45,322
3 Chapman & Co.	1,290
4 Derek Inc.	7,864
5 Erica spa	11,543
6 Fratelli	6,543
7 Groves Ltd	3,211
8 Horrobin & Sons	9,867
9 IMD Ltd	3,345
10 Jacksonville Import Co.	5,436
11 Kleinfeld	998
12 Lovesey Ltd	4,567
13 Moroni	3,211
14 Newsome & Co.	8,760
15 O'Reilly	2,344
16 Parker Ltd	7,500
17 Quentin	1,290
18 Roberts Bros	6,155
19 Sullivan Storage	8,355
20 Tolley & Son	4,350
21 Underwood Ltd	12,346
22 Villanova	9,100
23 Walkers	6,767
24 Young Ltd	4,433
25 ZJQ Warehousing	7,651
TOTAL	£193,482

7.3 Results of debtors circularization received by 1 October

(a) BALANCES AGREED

1	Archer
3	Chapman
4	Derek
6	Fratelli
7	Groves
9	IMD
11	Kleinfeld
12	Lovesey
14	Newsome
15	O'Reilly
16	Parker
17	Quentin
20	Tolley
23	Walkers

(b) DISAGREED

	£
5 Erica	
Balance per W	11,543
Cheque sent by Erica	
28.8.X7	1,400
Balance per Erica	10,143
8 Horrobin	
Balance per W	9,867
Goods returned 15.8.X7 — credit requested	4,800
Balance per Horrobin	5,067
18 Roberts Bros	
Balance Per W	6,155

'This balance relates to moneys retained by us to cover any rectification work required on the warehouse installation carried out for us by W. Since the installation was completed, we have spent £7,000 on making good defects which we consider the responsibility of W. We therefore deny that £6,155 is now due to W.'

(c) NO REPLY RECEIVED

 2   *Bowers**
10   *Jacksonville Import Co.***
13   *Moroni*
19   *Sullivan Storage***
21   *Underwood**
22   *Villanova*
24   *Young Ltd***
25   *ZJQ Warehousing*

* *Both these replied that they maintain purchase ledgers in 'open item' form — i.e. they list only those invoices currently payable. They were therefore unable to state what balance was due to W at a past date.*
** *These are US customers.*

QUESTIONS FOR DISCUSSION

1. On the basis of the results of the interim tests, what further work needs to be done in order to ensure that W's debtors are correctly stated and recoverable?
2. Comment on the basis of selection of the debtors circularization sample.
3. What further action (if any) should the auditors take in response to the results of Tests 3 and 4?

Relevant reading

ICAEW Statements on Auditing and Reporting 901: *Verification of debtor balances: confirmation by direct communication*
SAS 300: *Accounting and internal control systems and audit risk assessments*
(APC Auditing Guideline 204: *Internal controls*)
SAS 400: *Audit evidence*
(APC Auditing Guideline 203: *Audit evidence*)

Case 8
Britlings Brewery

BACKGROUND

Britlings Brewery (BB) is a relatively small, independent brewing company based in Sheffield, where the brewery and head office are located. Britlings owns 270 public houses in Yorkshire and Lincolnshire, all of which are run by managers. Its year-end is 31 December and its auditors are carrying out the interim audit in October 19X9 for the December 19X9 year-end.

DOCUMENTS

8.1 Summary of fixed assets at 30 September 19X9 (£000)

(i) LAND AND BUILDINGS

	Brewery and offices	Freehold and long leasehold	Short leasehold
Cost or valuation (1.1.X9)	2,000	59,000	14,000
Additions	100	11,000	300
Disposals	–	(3,000)	(1,700)
Cost or valuation (30.9.×9)	2,100	67,000	12,600
Accumulated depreciation (1.1.X9)	12	–	70
Charge for year	4	–	6
Disposals	–	–	(2)
Accumulated depreciation (30.9.X9)	16	–	74

(ii) OTHER TANGIBLE FIXED ASSETS

	Plant and equipment	Furniture & fittings	Motor vehicles
Cost at 1.1.X9	1,535	11,500	2,500
Additions	350	4,500	600
Disposals	(140)	(2,300)	(340)
Cost at 30.9.X9	1,745	13,700	2,760

43

Accumulated depreciation			
(1.1.X9)	235	825	1,500
Charge for year	85	100	520
Disposals	(25)	(50)	(290)
Accumulated depreciation			
(30.9.X9)	295	875	1,730

No further major additions or disposals (individually > £50,000) are scheduled to take place before the year-end.

8.2   Analysis of fixed asset movements

	£000
Additions represent:	
Brewery − enlargement of bottling area	100
Freehold and long leasehold:	
Purchase of 12 properties	7,000
Additions and refurbishments to existing properties (9 projects)	4,000
	11,000
Short leasehold − additions and refurbishments	300
Plant and equipment:	
Brewery bottling plant	190
Office computerization	70
Other items (none individually > £50,000)	90
	350
Furniture and fittings:	
Office improvements	200
Pubs − 15 major projects	3,900
Pubs − other replacements, renewals	400
	4,500
Vehicles:	
Lorries	100
Managers' cars (70 cars)	500
	600

Disposals represent:

6 freehold/long leasehold properties	3,000

8 short leaseholds	1,700

Plant and equipment:

Old bottling plant	80
Old computer equipment	40
Sundry minor items	20
	140

Furniture and fittings – from pubs	2,300

Vehicles – 53 cars	340

8.3 Extract from Britlings Brewery's accounts for the year ended 31 December 19X8

ACCOUNTING POLICIES

Properties owned by the company are subject to valuation by chartered surveyors employed by the company. The last such valuation took place in 19X7. Other fixed assets are valued at cost.

Depreciation is provided as follows:

1. Freehold offices and industrial premises – over their estimated useful lives.
2. Freehold land – nil.
3. Freehold licensed premises – nil.
4. Leasehold land and buildings – over the terms of the leases.
5. Brewing equipment – over twenty years.
6. Other plant – over ten years.
7. Office equipment – over five years.
8. Vehicles – over five years.

It is the company's policy to maintain licensed premises in a state of repair such that the value of those properties does not diminish over time. The cost of this maintenance is charged to profits in the year in which it occurs. As a result, it is the opinion of the directors that any depreciation of licensed properties would be immaterial and accordingly no depreciation charge has been made.

8.4   Extract from permanent audit file: notes on fixed asset system

PROPERTIES

Major expenditure on properties, either the acquisition of a new pub or a large development or refurbishment project, has to be approved via a capital sanction. This is a detailed summary of the expenditure to be incurred and is prepared by the surveyor's department and approved by the board of directors. Each sanction is given a code number. See sample attached at A.

Orders for work, supplies etc. are issued by purchasing department, quoting the code number.

When individual invoices are received, they are linked with the original order and approved as follows:

Expenditure <£1,000 − surveyor
Expenditure >£1,000 − financial accountant
Expenditure >£5,000 − finance director
Expenditure >£50,000 − board of directors

and are then coded to the appropriate capital sanction. A quarterly summary is prepared by the financial accountant comparing actual with budgeted expenditure and is reviewed by the board. See B for example. All disposals of properties must be approved by the board of directors.

Each property is allotted a code number and recorded in the Estates Register, a computerized listing of properties, which records both the original purchase and the cost of additions and alterations.

All freehold property deeds and copies of lease agreements are held at head office and filed by code number. A register is kept in which details of issues and returns of deeds (e.g. to/from solicitors) are noted.

PLANT AND EQUIPMENT

This includes brewing vessels and equipment, computers and other office machinery and beer storage and dispensing equipment at pubs. A computerized fixed asset register is maintained. Every asset capitalized and not fully depreciated is included on the register, identified by a unique code number which is also recorded on the asset itself. The register also calculates depreciation.

Additions to plant and equipment must be sanctioned by the manager of the department concerned. Items costing more than £1,000 must be approved by the financial accountant and those over £5,000 by the finance director. Items over £50,000 must be sanctioned by the board of directors.

It is company policy to write off items with a value < £100 to expenses. Disposals must be sanctioned by the manager of the department concerned. Disposals of items with proceeds or net book value in excess of £5,000 must be sanctioned by the finance director.

VEHICLES

These comprise beer delivery lorries and tankers and the cars provided to pub managers and senior managers within the company. Registration documents are retained by the fleet manager, who authorizes all purchases and disposals of vehicles up to £50,000.

A: EXAMPLE OF CAPITAL SANCTION

LOCATION   King's Arms, Bruddersford

PROJECT   Extend and refurbish bars

START DATE   1 March 19X9

ESTIMATED DURATION   2 months

BUDGETED COSTS	£
Architect's fees	4,500
Building labour and materials	71,000
Plant hire	3,800
Painting and decoration	11,000
Furniture	19,000
Carpeting	4,690
Fittings	9,540
Total	123,530

B: EXAMPLE OF QUARTERLY EXPENDITURE SUMMARY

LOCATION   White Rose, Darrowby

PROJECT   Build restaurant and conservatory

START DATE   31 March 19X9

ESTIMATED DURATION   6 months

REPORT DATE   30 June 19X9

	BUDGET	ACTUAL
	£	£
Architect's fees	5,000	5,100
Building labour and materials	55,000	39,000
Plant hire	3,900	2,300
Painting and decoration	12,000	–
Furniture	20,000	–
Carpeting	7,000	–
Fittings	9,500	–
Total	112,400	46,400

QUESTIONS FOR DISCUSSION

1. Describe and evaluate the effectiveness of the company's system for controlling additions to and disposals of fixed assets.
2. Suggest tests for verifying:
   (a) that land and buildings exist and are owned by the company;
   (b) that their value is fairly stated;
   (c) that plant and equipment exists and its value is fairly stated;
   (d) that vehicles exist and are owned by the company.

Relevant reading

SAS 300: *Accounting and internal control systems and audit risk assessments* (APC Auditing Guideline 204: *Internal controls*)

Case 9
Mrs Beeton's Kitchens Limited

BACKGROUND

Mrs Beeton's Kitchens Ltd (MBK) specializes in the design and installation of fitted kitchens. Fitting consultants visit a customer's home, measure the kitchen and quote a price based on the type of units and electrical appliances selected by the customer. MBK buys in the appliances – cookers, refrigerators, dishwashers, etc. – from the manufacturers, and also buys fittings such as sinks and taps. It makes the kitchen units, counters and shelves in its own workshop. A kitchen can cost from £3,000 to £10,000, depending on the type and number of units and appliances installed. Customers are required to pay a 20 per cent deposit when they place their order, and the balance is payable when the work is completed. It is July 19X9 and MBK's auditors are currently carrying out the audit for the year ending 30 June 19X9.

DOCUMENTS

9.1 Draft summary of creditors and accruals for the year ended 30 June 19X9

	19X9 £	19X8 £
Purchase ledger balance	359,087	238,566
Bank overdraft	100,235	76,897
Bank loan	25,000	–
Accruals:		
Goods received not invoiced*	84,950	100,500
PAYE and NI	37,000	29,000
VAT	55,000	39,000
Light and heat	30,000	37,000
Telephone	3,000	2,300
Sundry	11,000	21,000
Customer deposits received	16,500	12,500
	721,772	556,763

* Stores dept makes a list of items received in the last week of the financial year for which invoices are unlikely to be received until after the balance sheet date. The estimated value of those items is used as a basis for the 'goods received not invoiced' figure.

9.2   Draft profit and loss account for the year ended 30 June 19X9

	19X9	19X8
	£000	£000
Turnover	10,400	7,300
Wages	3,200	2,900
Materials	1,230	1,000
Appliances	3,000	2,000
Fittings	420	220
Gross profit	2,550	1,180
Salaries	600	450
Light and heat	230	180
Depreciation	220	190
Telephone and stationery	100	70
Motor expenses	110	80
Interest and bank charges	70	45
	1,220	165

9.3   Purchase ledger systems notes

1.   An order is raised by the Buying Department, based on a requisition from the department requiring the item. The order is sequentially numbered and produced in a carbon set with 4 copies:
– top copy to supplier
– copy retained by Buying Dept
– copy to department making the requisition
– copy to goods receiving department
Managers are subject to authority limits in signing order requisitions. Individual limits are:
– departmental manager: £5,000
– financial director: £20,000
– managing director: £50,000
– main board: all amounts over £50,000

2.   When the goods are received, the accompanying delivery note is compared with the order to ensure the goods are correct and is marked with the order number. The order is then stamped 'GOODS RECEIVED' and sent to the purchase ledger department and filed there in number order. The delivery note is sent to the Buying Department and filed there in alphabetical order of supplier name.

3.   The supplier's invoice is sent to the purchase ledger department where it is matched with the stamped order. (Suppliers are requested to quote MBK's order number on their invoices.) A purchase ledger clerk reviews the invoice to check that:

- price, type and quantity of goods invoiced agree with order;
- supplier is one of the company's authorized suppliers;
- the invoice is arithmetically correct.

The clerk then initials the invoice to indicate approval and enters on it the relevant purchase ledger and nominal ledger codes to which it is to be posted. If an invoice is denominated in a foreign currency, she translates it into £ sterling at the prevailing exchange rate for the day on which she processes it.

Where no purchase order exists, e.g. for utilities or professional services, the invoice is passed to the departmental manager concerned, who signs it to indicate authorization (subject to the limits noted in 1 above) and returns it.

4. The invoice is then passed to the data input clerk, who enters it into the computer in accordance with the codes indicated and returns it to purchase ledger department for filing in alphabetical order of supplier.

5. When the invoice is input, it simultaneously updates:
- the purchase ledger
- the nominal ledger
- the purchase invoice listing.

6. Once a month, the computer produces a listing of purchase ledger balances, showing the amount payable to each supplier and the invoices making it up. The financial accountant reviews the listing and marks on it the amounts to be paid to each supplier, e.g. the whole amount, all invoices more than 2 months old, etc. This is done in order to optimize the company's cash position by paying creditors only when it is desirable or essential, e.g. in order to obtain discounts or to ensure further orders are accepted.

7. The marked listing is then passed to the cashier, who inputs the information to the computer. The computer run:
- prints cheques to the suppliers concerned;
- prints a remittance advice, to be sent out with the cheque, stating which invoices it is paying;
- updates the cash book;
- updates the purchase ledger;
- updates the cash account in the nominal ledger.

The cheques are signed by the financial director and sent out with remittance advices.

8. Until November 19X8, a purchase ledger clerk compared purchase ledger balances with the monthly statements sent out by suppliers and followed up any discrepancies. When the clerk left, she was not replaced, and there is currently no review of suppliers' statements.

9. If goods are returned to a supplier because they are defective, they are accompanied by a goods return note. This is sequentially numbered and recorded in a goods return book which shows the goods involved, their order number and the supplier to whom they were returned. The stamped order copy is attached to the carbon of the goods return note and both are retained

in the stores until a replacement for the goods is received, when the order is processed as described in 2 above.

9.4 Summary of purchase ledger balances at 30 June 19X9

BALANCES INDIVIDUALLY >£10,000:

	Notes	£
Ruritanian Electrical	*1*	*100,090*
Breckland Timber		*45,800*
Perrys Plumbing Supplies		*12,346*
Plastitops Ltd		*15,500*
Ace Carpentry Supplies		*16,754*
Lave-Vaisselle	*2*	*68,765*
Freezomat Refrigerators		*28,760*
		288,015
75 other balances		*71,072*
(largest £9,000, smallest £3)		
		359,087

NOTES
1. *MBK imports all the cookers it sells from Ruritania. Ruritanian Electrical invoices it in the local currency, the rudolf. MBK cannot buy rudolfs forward, as a result of exchange restrictions. During the year, the value of the rudolf has increased from £1 = 50R to £1 = 40R.*
2. *Lave-Vaisselle is a French company which supplies MBK with dishwashers. It invoices MBK in £ sterling.*

9.5 Extract from systems audit working papers for the year ended 30 June 19X9

Purchases Test 1

Objective: *To ensure that recorded liabilities represent goods or services which have been received by the company.*

Work done: *Selected a representative sample of 30 purchase invoices posted to the purchase ledger between July 19X8 and June 19X9. For each invoice, ensured that:*
– the invoice had been initialled by the purchase ledger clerk
– the invoice details were in agreement with the copy order
– the copy order had been stamped 'GOODS RECEIVED'
or, where the invoice was for services, ensured that it had been approved by an authorized person.

Results: *See attached for details.* [NB: Not included in case study.] *No errors were found.*

Conclusion: *Recorded liabilities represent goods or services which have been received by the company.*

Test 2

Objective: *To ensure that goods or services cannot be received without a liability being recorded.*

Work done: *Selected a representative sample of 30 delivery notes from those filed in the Buying Dept and ensured that the liability to which they related had been posted to the purchase ledger. This was done by tracing details from delivery notes held in Buying Dept to orders, thence to stamped orders and invoices and tracing the invoices to the purchase ledger, ensuring that the correct amount had been posted to the correct supplier and in the correct period.*

Results:

	SUPPLIER	DELIVERY DATE	INVOICE SEEN	POSTED TO P.L.
1	Perrys	1 July	Y	Y
2	Abco	16 July	Y	Y
3	Ace	29 July	Y	Y
4	Walker	5 Aug	Y	Y
5	Freezo	13 Aug	Y	Y
6	Martin	28 Aug	Y	Y
7	Premier	3 Sept	Y	Y
8	Bird Ltd	11 Sept	Y	Y
9	McBride	19 Sept	Y	Y
10	Hayes Ltd	1 Oct	Y	Y
11	Perks & Co	20 Oct	Y	Y
12	Tompkins	29 Oct	Y	Y
13	James Ltd	3 Nov	Y	Y
14	Porter	17 Nov	Y	Y
15	Jessop plc	2 Dec	Y	Y
16	SJ Industries	22 Dec	Y	Y
17	Ruritanian	7 Jan	Y	Y
18	Mead	30 Jan	Y	Y
19	Shearer Ltd	8 Feb	Y	Y
20	O'Ryan	16 Feb	Y	Y

21	Khan Ltd	14 Mar	Y	Y
22	Campbell	29 Mar	Y	Y
23	Franklin & Co.	4 Apr	Y	Y
24	Henry	13 Apr	N	N
25	XL Products	6 May	Y	Y
26	Breckland	17 May	Y	Y
27	Plastitops	31 May	Y	N
28	Miller Bros	11 Jun	Y	Y
29	PK Plumbing	14 Jun	Y	N
30	Lave-Vaisselle	26 Jun	N	N

(Y = yes, N = no)

'No' answers can be explained as follows:

Henry — purchase ledger dept have investigated this and have come to the conclusion that the invoice must have been mislaid. They will write to the supplier and request a duplicate.

Plastitops — this invoice has not been posted to the purchase ledger because of a query by MBK about the price charged. It will be posted when the price has been agreed with the supplier.

PK Plumbing — the invoice is still (20 July) with the Contracts Manager for approval.

Lave-Vaisselle — invoice not yet received. Apparently there is normally a delay of 4 weeks between Lave-Vaisselle's delivery of goods and sending an invoice.

[...]

QUESTIONS FOR DISCUSSION

1. Test 2 above is incomplete. Suggest what conclusions the auditor might have drawn from it.
2. What final audit tests might be performed to test whether the following are completely and correctly stated:
   (a) purchase ledger balance;
   (b) bank overdraft;
   (c) bank loan;
   (d) goods received not invoiced?

Relevant reading

APC Auditing Guideline 401: *Bank reports for audit purposes*

Case 10
Golden Foods Limited

BACKGROUND

Golden Foods (GF) Ltd makes pies, pastries and pizzas, which it sells to retailers under its own brand-name and also supplies to a major supermarket chain. It has two sites: the bakery and its head office at Darlington, and a distribution depot in Wolverhampton.

GF's year-end is 31 March 19X9 and its accounts are required to be ready for publication by 30 May. It is now 19 May and the final audit work is due to be completed by 20 May. The manager in charge of the audit is reviewing the audit file with a view to identifying any unresolved problems.

(You may assume that an interim audit has been performed, and that its results were satisfactory except for any deficiencies specifically mentioned in the case study.)

DOCUMENTS

10.1 Summary of results

	19X9	19X8
	£000	£000
Turnover	3,768	3,477
Gross profit	1,240	1,199
Gross profit %	32.9	34.5
Net profit	208	189
Fixed assets	1,100	1,005
Stock	140	195
Debtors	712	597
Bank balances	43	51
Current liabilities	(433)	(494)
Net assets	1,562	1,354
Share capital	1,100	1,100
Reserves	462	254
Shareholders' funds	1,562	1,354

10.2   Stock summary

	19X9 £000	19X8 £000
At Darlington:		
Finished products	43	61
Raw materials	41	48
Packing materials	38	47
At Wolverhampton:		
Finished products	18	39
Total	140	195

NOTES:

The following audit work has been carried out on the stock at Darlington:
- *attended physical stocktake held on 31 March and performed test counts;*
- *ensured that material items of stock had been valued at the lower of cost and net realizable value;*
- *ensured that none of the stock on hand at 31 March was damaged or out of condition.*

The results of all tests were satisfactory.

Because of staff shortages, a physical count was not performed at Wolverhampton. The stock figure was extracted from the stock records maintained at the depot. The audit team paid a one-day visit to the Wolverhampton depot, in the course of which it performed the following audit work:
- *agreed the stock balance in the accounts to the stock records;*
- *discussed the year-end stock figure with the depot manager and ascertained that he considered the figure to be reasonable and that in his opinion year-end stock did not require any provision for obsolete/damaged items.*

10.3   Summary of debtors

	19X9 £000	19X8 £000
Trade debtors	535	498
Loan to related company	120	20
Prepayments	57	79
Total	712	597

10.4   Summary of results of debtors circularization

WORK DONE
A sample of 48 debtors was circularized. This represented all balances >£10,000 at 31 March and a representative sample of 25 others. A reminder letter was sent to all who had not replied by 1 May.

RESULTS
Results were as follows, on the basis of replies received up to 18 May.

	Notes	£000	No.	% of value
Agreed		109	18	30
Reconciled	1	140	14	37
Disagreed	2	31	1	8
No reply		95	15	25
Total		375	48	100

NOTES:
1. Reconciling items were due to differences between the dates at which invoices and payments were entered in customers' and in GF's records.
2. The disagreement relates to an invoice for £3,000 sent to this customer in December 19X8. The customer is refusing to pay, on the grounds that the goods were damaged in transit.

CONCLUSION
As only £109K of debtor balances out of a total of £535K have been confirmed, it is not possible to conclude whether or not debtors are correctly stated.

10.5   Loan to associated company

This is an unsecured loan made to Bartleby Ltd, a company in which GF owns 10% of the share capital. GF loaned Bartleby £20K in 19X8 to provide working capital, and this amount has now been increased to £120K. No repayments have been received. The finance director of GF was unwilling for us to include this balance in our circulation of debtors. Accordingly, audit work has been confined to the following:
— agreed balance outstanding to the nominal ledger;
— traced payment to cash book, bank statement and returned cheque and ensured the cheque payee is Bartleby;
— discussed the balance with Mrs Bateman, the finance director, who stated that in her opinion it is fully recoverable.

10.6   Fixed assets

All figures £000

COST	1.4.X8	Addns	Disposals	31.3.X9
Freehold land & buildings	600	200	—	800
Plant	2,000	1,000	700	2,300
Motor vehicles	300	700	200	800
Fixtures & fittings	105	200	5	300
Total	3,005	2,100	905	4,200

DEPRECIATION	1.4.X8	For year	Disposals	31.3.X9
Freehold buildings	125	20	—	145
Plant	1,575	850	60	2,365
Motor vehicles	250	250	35	465
Fixtures & fittings	50	80	5	125
Total	2,000	1,200	100	3,100

NET BOOK VALUE	1,005			1,100

Notes
(1) The addition to land and buildings is in fact the surplus arising on revaluation. This revaluation was carried out by one of the directors of GF, who is a chartered surveyor.
(2) The figure for additions to plant has been overstated. A number of orders for items of plant not received at the year-end have been accrued instead of being treated as capital commitments. As a result, fixed assets and current liabilities have both been overstated by £75K.

QUESTIONS FOR DISCUSSION

Assuming that the results of the audit were satisfactory in all other areas:

1. Identify the unresolved problems which the audit manager has to clear. What is the potential impact of each on the financial statements?
2. Suggest how each of the problems might be resolved by the audit team and/or GF's management in the time available. The alternatives might include:
   (a) altering the accounts;

(b) qualifying the audit report;
(c) obtaining management assurances in the letter of representation
(d) performing additional audit work.
In each case you should be specific about the steps to be taken (e.g. what tests are to be performed, what audit qualification is needed, etc.).

Relevant reading

SAS 440: *Management representations*
(APC Auditing Guideline 404: *Representations by management*)
SAS 520: *Using the work of an expert*
(APC Auditing Guideline 413: *Reliance on other specialists*)

Case 11
Massive Motors Limited

BACKGROUND

Massive Motors Ltd (MM) is part of the Massive Group plc, which has a consolidated turnover of £200 million. MM operates a chain of garages throughout the UK which sell petrol and carry out repairs and services. Three of the garages also deal in new and second-hand cars. MM is a UK dealer for Eagle cars, which are imported from Ruthenia. Its year-end is 31 March.

Jill White is the audit partner in charge of the MM audit. The 19X8 audit fieldwork has just been completed, and Jill is reviewing the file in order to establish whether any additional work needs to be done and to identify matters for discussion with MM's financial director at their closing audit meeting, which is due to be held tomorrow.

DOCUMENTS

11.1   Draft summarized accounts for MM for the year ended 31 March 19X8

	£000
TURNOVER:	
Petrol	*6,140*
Repairs and services	*1,500*
Car sales	*4,350*
TOTAL	*11,990*
COST OF SALES	*7,300*
GROSS MARGIN	*4,690*
EXPENSES	*2,150*
NET PROFIT BEFORE TAX	*2,540*
FIXED ASSETS	
Land & buildings	*4,500*
Plant	*1,200*
Fixtures & fittings	*500*
Vehicles	*600*
	6,800

CURRENT ASSETS

Stock	4,075
Debtors & prepayments	1,640
Bank & cash	125
	5,840

CURRENT LIABILITIES

Creditors & accruals	1,100
Bank loan	3,000
	4,100

NET CURRENT ASSETS	1,740
NET ASSETS	8,540

REPRESENTED BY:

Share capital	5,000
Profit & loss account	2,540
Revaluation reserve	1,000
	8,540

11.2 Extract from 19X8 audit file

LAND AND BUILDINGS

MM owns 5 freehold garages and its head office building in Barchester; it does not own any leaseholds. Land and buildings are valued in the balance sheet on the basis of an independent valuation carried out by a firm of surveyors in 19X7. Values of individual sites are as follows:

	£000
Barchester	875
Stoke	1,050
Cardiff	760
Dundee	635
Bristol	580
Leeds	600
Total	4,500

Recently (June 19X8), MM's management has commissioned another independent valuation. They do not intend to incorporate the results in the 19X8 financial statements as they were notified after the year-end. The revaluation is summarized below.

	£000
Barchester	*975*
Stoke	*850*
Cardiff	*1,060*
Dundee	*785*
Bristol	*980*
Leeds	*650*
Total	*5,300*

At 31 March, MM had contracted with Newtown Properties plc to purchase a site in Newtown and with the Betta Building Co. Ltd for the construction of a garage and car showroom there. The site is expected to cost £500K and the building work c. £275K.

11.3 Extracts from minutes of the meeting of the board of directors of MM Ltd, held on 31 March 19X8 at MM House, Barchester

Agenda Item 6: Capital investments

On receiving a report from the Capital Investment Subcommittee, the board authorized the purchase of the following:

	Authorized price £
1 breakdown recovery lorry	10,000
3 Ford Sierra cars for sales managers	30,000
Equipment for installation at Cardiff, as specified on attached schedule	18,000

Agenda Item 7: Legal claim by Identical Copiers Ltd

The company secretary reported that he had contacted the company's solicitors on 24 March, and they had confirmed that Identical Copiers were proceeding with their claim for damages against MM. The solicitors recommended that MM should proceed to give them instructions so that they could proceed as soon as possible with their related case against Flitwick Motor Spares Ltd. After some discussion, it was agreed that the company secretary, together with Mr Goodwood, the Operations Director, should prepare a detailed report for discussion at the next board meeting.

Agenda Item 10: Guarantee to Caledonian Bank Ltd

The seal of the company was affixed to a guarantee given to the Caledonian Bank Ltd by the company in respect of the £1.5M loan made by the Bank to Massive Manufacturing Ltd.

11.4 Extract from 19X8 audit file: note of a meeting with Mr Alan Chivers, Company Secretary of MM Ltd, on 15 March 19X8

PRESENT: A. Chivers – Company Secretary
 B. Bryant – Audit Senior

I explained that I had asked to see Mr Chivers in order to discuss the possible existence of any outstanding legal matters which needed to be reflected in MM's accounts. Mr Chivers stated that as company secretary he was responsible for all the company's legal affairs. The only matter currently outstanding was the suit for damages being brought against the company by Identical Copiers (IC) of Bristol.

IC was a small company which provided a copier repair service and guaranteed that all customers within 25 miles of Bristol city centre would receive a visit from an IC repairman within 2 hours of calling the company. IC used a fleet of 5 vans to call on customers.

In the first week of October 19X7, the MM garage in Bristol carried out a service and overhaul of all IC's vans. In the fortnight that followed, all the vans successively broke down. They proved to need major engine repairs, which meant that IC was without any vans for 2 working days and operating with a skeleton fleet for a further 5 days. During this time, IC was unable to honour its guarantee of service within 2 hours. As a result, it lost several customers, including a major customer to whom it had made 30% of its sales in its first year of trading. IC went into liquidation in January 19X8 as a result of the losses it had sustained.

Mr Frank Thorn, the managing director of IC and its major shareholder, is suing MM for damages of £250K. He claims that the company's liquidation was caused by the loss of its fleet of vans and that the vans had been damaged by MM's installation of defective parts when they carried out the service in October 19X7. MM's costs are estimated at £30K.

MM does not dispute the facts of the case. It considers, however, that the ultimate liability for the damage suffered by IC lies with Flitwick Motor Spares Ltd, from whom it purchased the parts used on the IC vehicles. MM intends to bring a claim for damages against Flitwick for their negligence in supplying defective parts, and this claim will be for the amount of damages claimed by IC together with MM's own legal costs.

Mr Chivers considers that there is no need for MM to disclose IC's claim in the 19X8 accounts, as the likely outcome of the cases will have a net effect of nil on MM's results – the damages paid to IC will be balanced out by those recovered from Flitwick. He also considers that disclosure would be damaging to MM, both by prejudging the outcome of the IC case, which could conceivably go in MM's favour, and by giving Flitwick advance warning that MM intends to bring an action against them.

11.5   Reply to bank confirmation request sent by auditors

30 April 19X8

Dear Sirs

MASSIVE MOTORS LTD

In response to your letter dated 2 April 19X8, we wish to report the following in respect of our above customer:

BANK ACCOUNTS IN CUSTOMER'S NAME:
A/C No. 10009876: Balance at 31 March 19X8 100,000 Ruthenian dinars

No other accounts in this name existed during the year.

CUSTOMER'S ASSETS HELD AS SECURITY:
None

CUSTOMER'S OTHER ASSETS HELD:
None

CONTINGENT LIABILITIES:
Outstanding forward foreign exchange contracts:
£100,000 for delivery of 50,000 Ruthenian dinars on 1 July 19X8
£100,000 for delivery of 55,000 Ruthenian dinars on 1 September 19X8

This reply is given solely for the purpose of your audit without any responsibility to you on the part of the bank, its employees or agents, but it is not to relieve you from any other inquiry or from the performance of any other duty.

Yours faithfully

R. Singh
Manager, Cheapside Branch

Audit note: at 31 March 19X8, £1 = 0.5 Ruthenian dinar

11.6   Extract from 19X8 audit file: contingent liabilities

As a promotional exercise, MM gave a 12-month warranty on all second-hand cars it sold during the year ending 31 March 19X8. Under the warranty, it will provide free repairs on all cars it supplied (with the exclusion of repairs to windscreens and tyres) in respect of any defect arising within 12 months of the date of sale.

During 19X7/8 MM sold 1,500 used cars, representing a turnover of £4.5M. According to its costing records, which we have reviewed, the average cost of a repair job (comprising labour, parts and allocation of overhead but excluding any mark-up) was £125.

MM proposes to disclose this as a contingent liability in the notes to the accounts.

QUESTIONS FOR DISCUSSION

1. Identify the issues in these working papers which might be described as:
   (a) post-balance sheet events;
   (b) commitments;
   (c) contingencies.
2. For each issue, comment on:
   (a) the accounting treatment/disclosure proposed by MM. Do you consider it to be correct? If not, what treatment/disclosure would you suggest?
   (b) the audit work done. Is it adequate? If not, what additional work do you consider necessary?

Relevant reading

Accounting Standards Committee SSAP 17: *Accounting for post balance sheet events*
Accounting Standards Committee SSAP 18: *Accounting for contingencies*
APC Auditing Guideline 401: *Bank reports for audit purposes*
ICAEW Statements on Auditing and Reporting 903: *The ascertainment and confirmation of contingent liabilities arising from pending legal matters*
SAS 150: *Subsequent events*
(APC Auditing Guideline 402: *Events after the balance sheet date*)

Case 12
Holiday Holdings Limited

BACKGROUND

Holiday Holdings Ltd (HH) is a group of companies in the leisure industry. Its subsidiaries include Lyndon Hotel Ltd and the Park Leisure Complex Ltd.

Because of pressure on audit fees, the auditors of HH are anxious to reduce the time taken to carry out their substantive audit testing during the 19X9 audit. One means of doing this which they wish to use is that of analytical review. The audit senior, Susan Grey, has collected data on two areas which she considers suitable for analytical review: turnover for room lettings at the hotel, and wages and salaries at the leisure complex.

DOCUMENTS

12.1   Lyndon Hotel: Extract from permanent audit file

The hotel has 3 main sources of income: the bar, the restaurant and room lettings. It maintains separate cash and nominal accounts for all these activities. Where a guest's bill includes charges for two different categories, e.g. room and bar, the sales are subsequently re-analysed by the hotel's accountant to post the appropriate amounts to the correct accounts.

The hotel has 100 bedrooms, all of which are double rooms, but which are also let for single occupancy. The room rate for 19X9 is £25 if the room is let to one person and £30 if it is let to two people. The fact that the room rate is higher for double than for single occupancy makes it important that guests are correctly invoiced, i.e. that a room occupied by two people is charged at the double rate. The receptionist who prepares the invoice for a guest on departure is required to check the rate charged against the booking confirmation, to ensure that the correct rate has been used.

In addition to a monthly profit and loss account, the hotel accountant produces statistics for management information which show room occupancy, i.e. the % of rooms used, and bed occupancy, i.e. the average use of beds during the month. For instance:

Available bed nights in May = 31 days × 200 beds = 6,200

If 2,540 bed nights were sold, May occupancy = 41%

If all rooms are let for single occupancy, the maximum bed occupancy is 50%.

These statistics are based on the data taken at the time of booking, not on the invoiced amounts.

12.2 Summary of occupancy statistics for year ending 30 April 19X9

	Room occupancy %	Bed occupancy %
May	65	41
June	67	48
July	71	56
August	70	51
September	65	52
October	63	47
November	60	44
December	57	45
January	57	46
February	61	52
March	58	43
April	63	47
Annual average	63	47.67

12.3 Extract from profit and loss account for the year ended 30 April 19X9

	19X9 £	19X8 £
TURNOVER		
Bar	435,000	400,987
Restaurant	367,589	349,876
Room letting	622,710	600,321
Total	1,425,299	1,351,184

12.4 Park Leisure Complex Ltd: Extract from 19X9 audit file

Park employs 50 weekly-paid and 10 monthly-paid (salaried) staff. Park has a pension scheme for its salaried employees, for whom it pays contributions calculated as 5% of their gross salary. There is no pension scheme for weekly-paid employees.

Weekly-paid employees are paid in cash. The payroll supervisor cashes the payroll cheque on Thursday of each week and pay packets are made up by her assistant to be distributed on Friday. Salaried employees are paid by bank transfer.

Both weekly- and monthly-paid employees received a 5% pay increase with immediate effect from 1 August 19X8.

The employer's national insurance contribution was 10.5% of earnings (excluding pension contributions) throughout the year.

Gross pay for a sample pay period was as follows:

Weekly-paid: week ending 7 May 19X8 £3,000 (including overtime).

Salaried: month ending 31 May 19X8 £4,580 (no overtime is payable to salaried staff).

The total cost of wages and salaries, including pension contributions and employer's NI, was £256,000 for the year ending 30 April 19X9.

QUESTIONS FOR DISCUSSION

1. Using the information given in the documents above:
   (a) Estimate the expected level of
   (i) income from room lettings;
   (ii) wages and salaries,
   for Lyndon and Park for the year ended 30 April 19X9.
   (b) Compare your results with the actual reported figures and suggest reasons for the difference.
   (c) What are the advantages and drawbacks of an analytical review approach to substantive testing?

Relevant reading

SAS 410: *Analytical procedures*
(APC Auditing Guideline 417: *Analytical review*)

Case 13
Fantasy Fashions Limited

BACKGROUND

Fantasy Fashions Ltd (Fantasy) is a private company manufacturing clothes which it sells wholesale. It has few accounting systems, so the audit by Pinkerton & Co. tends to be largely substantive. The accounts are prepared by Paul Stevens, who is accurate and conscientious, but tends to leave any accounting policy decisions to Jim Green, the managing director, a much more forceful character.

PEOPLE INVOLVED

Pinkerton & Co.
Arun Desai: Audit Partner
Jane Banks: Audit Manager
Sue Lloyd: Trainee

Fantasy
Jim Green: Managing Director
Paul Stevens: Accountant

DOCUMENTS

13.1   Pinkerton & Co. – Internal Memo

From: Jane Banks   *8 February 1995*
To: Sue Lloyd

FANTASY FASHIONS LTD
I looked at the files over the weekend. Everything seems OK to me, apart from stock. Can you write me a short note about those T-shirts?

13.2   Pinkerton & Co. – Internal Memo

From: Sue Lloyd
To: Jane Banks

FANTASY FASHIONS LTD
Year ended 31.12.94

STOCK SUMMARY

	1995 £	1994 £
Raw materials		
Cotton	9,180	6,537
Jersey	3,225	4,605
Thread, zips etc.	3,039	5,559
Finished goods		
jeans	–	10,797
overalls	–	20,700
T-shirts*	117,000	–
	132,444	48,198

* *These are 19,500 T-shirts which have been in stock since April 1994, when they were made for Giant Stores. I inspected them during the stocktake, and they appeared to be well made and in good condition. According to Mr Stevens, the accountant, they were rejected by Giant because the dye did not match other items in Giant's summer range. After an exchange of letters and visits lasting until September, Fantasy gave up the attempt to persuade Giant to pay for the T-shirts and accepted they were not up to the standard specified in the original agreement because of the dye fault.*

Fantasy did not try to find an alternative buyer during the summer, in the hope that Giant would relent. Mr Stevens tells me that a number of customers have expressed an interest in the garments this year, but he admits that no firm orders have been placed.

The T-shirts cost about £2.70 each to make, according to Mr Stevens. They have been valued in the accounts at £6 each, which was the agreed selling price to Giant.

13.3 Fantasy Fashions Ltd: Profit and Loss Account for the year ended 31 December 1995

	1995	1994
	£	£
Turnover	544,920	528,396
Operating costs	483,639	447,411
Operating profit	61,281	80,985
Interest payable	900	–
Profit before taxation	60,381	80,985
Taxation	24,000	28,500
RETAINED PROFIT	36,381	52,485

13.4 Fantasy Fashions Ltd: Balance sheet at 31 December 1995

	1995	1994
	£	£
FIXED ASSETS	100,500	75,000
CURRENT ASSETS		
Stock	132,444	48,198
Debtors	19,560	48,900
Bank and cash	2,250	39,000
	154,254	136,098
CURRENT LIABILITIES		
Bank overdraft	15,000	–
Trade creditors	29,025	32,250
Taxation	24,000	28,500
	68,025	60,750
NET CURRENT ASSETS	86,229	75,348
NET ASSETS	186,729	150,348
REPRESENTED BY		
Share capital	30,000	30,000
Reserves	156,729	120,348
	186,729	150,348

13.5   Pinkerton & Co. – Internal Memo

From: *Jane Banks*
To: *Arun Desai*   *10 February 1995*

FANTASY FASHIONS LTD
As you suggested, I went to see Jim Green yesterday to discuss stock valuation. Unfortunately, he went up the wall as soon as I mentioned it. When he calmed down a bit, he made the following points:

1.   *Giant has abused its dominant position by refusing to take up the T-shirts. If Fantasy had the resources, it would sue Giant and compel it to honour the contract. The difference between the dye quality specified and the actual colour of the T-shirts is tiny.*

2.   *If Fantasy had not wasted last summer negotiating with Giant, it would have been able to find another buyer for the T-shirts and this problem of year-end valuation would not have arisen.*

3.   *As director of Fantasy he is in any case better placed than the auditors to determine the value of his stock. He regards any questioning of his valuation as a sign that we do not trust him. He strongly hinted that he would consider a change of auditor if we could not 'reach an acceptable solution' – which I take to mean agreement to use his valuation.*

Anyway, I am leaving you the files and will be grateful for your comments.

Jane

13.5   Pinkerton & Co. – Internal Memo

From: *Arun Desai*
To: *Jane Banks*   *11 February 1995*

FANTASY FASHIONS LTD
Thanks for letting me see the files. Can you and Sue come to my office at 9.15 tomorrow? We need to discuss our next step.
A. D.

QUESTIONS FOR DISCUSSION

1. What further audit work, if any, should Pinkerton & Co carry out before drafting their audit report?
2. What should the wording of the audit report be and why?

Relevant reading

Accounting Standards Committee SSAP 9: *Stocks and long-term contracts*
SAS 600: *Auditors' reports on financial statements*

Case 14
Brighter Alloys Limited

BACKGROUND

Brighter Alloys Ltd (BA), a company based in the city of Bruddersford, deals in alloys used in the steel industry. It was founded in 1969 by Jack Brightman. In 1979 he and his family sold their shares in the company to Dickens Steel plc, and BA is now a wholly owned subsidiary of Dickens. Parker & Co. act as auditors of all the twelve companies in the Dickens Group, whose year-end is 31 December. From 1969 until 1987 Slott & Co., a small firm, were auditors of BA; the change of auditor was the decision of the finance director of Dickens.

DOCUMENTS

14.1 Summary accounts of Brighter Alloys 1986–1988

PROFIT AND LOSS ACCOUNT

£000	1986	1987	1988 (draft)
Turnover	2,150	2,325	2,200
Cost of sales	1,550	1,675	2,300
Gross margin	600	650	(100)
Admin expenses	100	108	120
Distribution expenses	147	160	170
Net profit/(loss)	353	382	(390)
Taxation	127	140	–
Profit/(loss) after tax	226	242	(390)
Dividend	175	200	–
Retained profit/(loss)	51	42	(390)

BALANCE SHEET

	1986	1987	1988
TANGIBLE FIXED ASSETS	700	720	740
CURRENT ASSETS			
Stocks	675	712	120
Debtors	300	350	365
Bank and cash	50	50	15
	1,025	1,112	500
CURRENT LIABILITIES			
Trade creditors	480	508	528
Overdraft	30	60	70
Taxation	150	132	–
Dividend	75	100	–
	735	800	598
Net current assets	290	312	(98)
Net assets	990	1,032	642
REPRESENTED BY			
Share capital	500	500	500
Profit & loss account	490	532	142
	990	1,032	642

14.2   Note on attendance at the stocktake of Brighter Alloys Ltd, 31 December 1988

I attended the stocktake of Brighter Alloys (BA), which took place on 31 December 1988, beginning at 9.00 a.m. BA's stock is kept at two locations. Scrap is kept in the yard outside BA's offices in Dundee Street. Alloy stores are held in a warehouse in Aberdeen Street, about half a mile from the offices. I arrived at Dundee Street at 8.30 a.m., and met Mrs Glenda White, the financial accountant of Dickens. She told me that she was attending the stocktake in the place of Jim Lodge, the managing director of BA, who was unwell. He had telephoned her the previous evening to say that he would not be present.

The stocktake was carried out by professional stocktakers from Sharp & Co.; Mr Lodge had offered BA staff to perform the work, but his offer had been rejected by Peter Hart, the new financial director of Dickens, who had requested the stocktake. Mr Hart felt that BA staff had insufficient stocktaking experience. Two teams of stocktakers were in action, one at each site where stock was held. Mrs White and I went to Aberdeen Street to observe the alloy stores count, which was expected to represent most of the stock value.

Alloy stores were held in drums, each containing half a tonne. The stocktakers at Aberdeen Street had selected a random sample of drums to be moved to one end of the yard so that their lids could be cut off and the contents inspected. When we arrived, the stocktaker immediately informed us that the first drum opened, which was labelled Monel 400, had proved to contain scrap and swarf with a thin top layer of Monel. The warehouse employee present could not offer any explanation for this. Two other drums opened also proved to be full of swarf.

The stocktakers had been provided with copies of BA's most recent stock figures as a basis for conducting the count. One of them commented that there appeared to be far fewer drums on site than the stock listing would suggest, and asked Mrs White if there had been substantial sales during late December which had not yet been entered in the stock records. She said that December sales had, in fact, been extremely poor, and that she could think of no reason for the apparent stock shortage. At this point, Mrs White telephoned Mr Hart and informed him of the problems that had been encountered. She suggested that the stocktakers be instructed to open and sample all sealed drums, and that all movements in and out of the warehouse be suspended until this had been done. He agreed with this approach and work proceeded accordingly. I remained on site for the rest of the day to observe the work being carried out. Because of the need to carry out analysis of samples, the stocktakers were unable to report a stock value until a week after the initial count.

The results of the stocktakers' work as notified to Dickens on 9 January can be summarized as follows:

	£000
Value of stock per latest stock listing	695
Value of stock as counted on 31 December	120
Shortfall	575
Reasons for shortfall:	
Stock on list not found at stocktake	330
Drums found to be wholly/partly filled with swarf and scrap	120
Stock found to be of lower specification than stated in stock records*	125
	575

* This was found during the sampling process. Details are given in full on the stocktaker's report, but the main differences were as follows:

Stainless 18−8 (£1,250/tonne) instead of stainless 316 (£2,000/tonne)

Monel 400 (£7,500/tonne) instead of Monel K-500 (£9,000/tonne).

14.3   Extract from *Bruddersford Daily Record*, 15 September 1989

I STOLE HALF A MILLION, ADMITS EX-STEEL BOSS LODGE

Jim Lodge, ex-managing director of Bruddersford steel firm Brighter Alloys, today pleaded guilty to defrauding his employers, Dickens Steel, of sums totalling more than half a million over the five years he had worked for them.

Lodge admitted to a series of frauds against Dickens which began shortly after his appointment to their subsidiary, Brighter Alloys. Lodge was responsible for keeping the company's books and used his position of trust to carry out a variety of frauds that benefited him, his friends and family. Local dealers Victory Metal Co., whose director Martin Thorn has already been sentenced for his part in the fraud, supplied Lodge with invoices for short or non-existent deliveries. Lodge authorized the invoices and passed them to Dickens for payment. Later, he and Thorn split Dickens's payments between them.

As Lodge found that this went unnoticed, he began to submit fake invoices to Dickens. They were apparently from a scrap supplier. The supplier did not exist; Lodge collected the cheques regularly from the accommodation address − in fact, a room over a shop − to which they were sent, and paid them into a bank account opened in the 'supplier's' name.

Lodge became concerned that the discrepancy between the amount of stock allegedly purchased and the amount actually on hand would become readily apparent. Victory began to make deliveries to Brighter of drums containing either worthless scrap or metals of a lower quality than that which they invoiced. In order to forestall any inquiries about invoices, Lodge sent a memo to accounting staff at Dickens asking them to process payments to Victory as a matter of urgency, in order to take advantage of a prompt payment discount.

Lodge had sole responsibility for keeping the stock records at Brighter Alloys. He told Dickens that he carried out a full stocktake every month and made sure that the stock records were accurate. Lodge's 'stocktakes' were only for show. He invented stock figures of his own that would ensure

Brighter Alloy's profits looked satisfactory. Occasionally Lodge would be asked about evident discrepancies between book stock and the goods at the warehouse. He would claim that these resulted from stock being in transit or at the firm's other site.

Brighter Alloy's auditors had traditionally accepted the stock figures supplied by the company. When new auditors Parker & Co. were appointed in 1987 by Dicken's new finance director they asked to attend stocktakes, but were deterred by Lodge, who claimed that he was too busy. He finally agreed − but he took care that the warehouse was arranged specially, with 'good' stock closest to the oxy-acetylene equipment needed to cut drums open. The oxy-acetylene pipe was deliberately shortened so that cutting equipment could not be used on the drums full of waste.

Lodge's downfall came in December 1988. Dicken's management was dissatisfied with Brighter Alloys' results, which had remained nearly static for the past few years. Peter Hart decided that the subsidiary should be sold off as soon as a buyer could be found. He insisted on a full stocktake as an aid to putting a value on the company. Hart suspected that Lodge was an inefficient manager − he blamed the company's poor results on this − and insisted on excluding him and his staff from taking part in the stock count. On the day of the count, Lodge was absent from work, claiming to be ill. He never returned to work. Within days of the stocktake, he was interviewed by the police in connection with the massive stock shortage which the stocktake had revealed. Lodge at first claimed that the company must have been burgled, but finally admitted his responsibility. He told police that the proceeds of his theft had been spent partly on his luxurious lifestyle, including a holiday home in Florida, performance cars and cabin cruiser, and partly on making good losses incurred by a business owned by his wife and son.

Lodge is due to be sentenced tomorrow.

14.4 Transcript of a meeting at the offices of Parker & Co., Bruddersford, on 31 March 1989

PRESENT: Walter Bell, senior partner (WB)
John Lee, partner in charge of the Dickens audit (JL)
Mark Clayton, manager on Dickens audit (MC)
Barry Scott, audit senior on Dickens audit (BS)

WB As you know, John and I are due to meet the board of Dickens next week to discuss the whole business of the fraud at Brighter Alloys. They are extremely unhappy and embarrassed about the losses the group has suffered. Hart, in particular, is very upset, as he feels the affair has undermined his credibility, and he is clearly anxious to lay as much of the blame as possible on the auditors' shoulders. Now my view is that we did all that could reasonably be expected of us on the Brighter audit, and we have nothing to reproach ourselves with − but we do need to get the facts clear so that John and I are fully briefed for our meeting. I'd like to begin by sorting out the history of Brighter up to the time we were appointed. Can you start us off, John?

JL Yes, certainly. Brighter was founded in 1969 and its auditors were Slott & Co., who were a small firm then and remained that way. Brighter expanded dramatically, especially in the mid-1970s and early 1980s, but they kept Slott as auditors. Slott seem to have done little for them apart from providing an audit and preparing tax returns, but they had a good relationship with the management. The Dickens board occasionally made noises about the need to have the same auditors for the parent and all its subsidiaries, but they never did anything about it. When Hart came along, he forced the issue. He thought the group could achieve savings on the audit fee by having the same auditors throughout, and he was looking for a more positive attitude than Slott were displaying. He wanted suggestions about ways in which Brighter could tighten up its systems and improve performance.

WB What kind of audit work did Slott do?

MC I reviewed their files when we took over. They did a lot of vouching work, agreeing entries in the ledgers to purchase invoices and so on for months at a time. But they didn't do what we'd call a system audit. I suppose there wasn't much of a system to test, though. Certainly the work was carried out meticulously, and all the queries were followed up with Lodge. But it was very limited in scope, and the same programme was followed every year, even to testing the same months' transactions.

BS Well, they didn't attend the stocktake. That was always carried out by the managing director: originally Brightman, then Johnson, who took over when Dickens acquired them, then finally Lodge. The MD produced stock sheets, which they agreed to the trial balance and the balance sheet. And that was about all.

WB   Did they ever make any comments in management letters?

JL   I discussed this with the partner in Slott & Co. who looked after them.
He said that if they had any problems, they always used to talk them over
with Jack Brightman face to face, and they kept up that tradition with
Johnson and then with Lodge. So they never put any comments in
writing.

WB   Mark, what were your impressions of Brighter when we took over the
audit? I mean in terms of the way it was managed and run?

MC   I knew that Hart wasn't happy about the efficiency of management, so I
was expecting to see a shambles. In fact, I have to admit I was quite
impressed with Lodge. He seemed to be on top of every aspect of the
business — he had figures for debtors, bank balances, stock, everything,
at his command. He was producing quarterly management accounts
and monitoring performance. I could see that performance wasn't up to
the targets Dickens had set, but it seemed to me that Lodge was working
flat out to turn the company round. And he did work very hard; never
took more than three or four days' holiday at a time and worked very
long hours. He used to tell us about the place he had in Florida and how
his wife went there on her own for holidays — he hadn't the time to go
with her.

WB   Didn't you find it odd that he had that, and ran a boat and various cars?
The salary from Brighter wasn't all that good.

JL   Mark and I discussed this once. We thought he did well — but he had told
us about the shops his wife and son ran, and we assumed that those paid
for the luxuries. And he'd had a high-powered job down south before he
came here. He might have had savings from that.

WB   Anyway, the first impression was that Lodge was making a fairly good
job of running Brighter, but that division of duty was non-existent?

MC   That's right. Barry can describe the way the office was run.

BS   Basically, Lodge did all the key jobs himself. He didn't control the bank
account; that was done centrally by Dickens. But he authorized all payments to suppliers and maintained the creditors ledger, so he could
approve the addition of new suppliers. His secretary opened the mail
and listed cheques; he did all the posting to the debtors ledger.

WB   So how did this affect stock?

BS   Lodge controlled stock all the way. The warehouse manager retired
shortly after Lodge joined, and he was never replaced. Lodge claimed that
it was a cost-cutting measure and that stock was so important that it
needed the involvement of senior management. So the staff at the warehouse were basically labourers who weren't likely to venture to criticize
what Lodge did.

WB   What was the stock system?

BS   The men at the warehouse kept delivery notes for goods received. When they made issues from stock, they made entries in a duplicate book. One copy of the page went with the goods; the other was sent to Lodge every week, along with that week's delivery notes. Lodge kept the stock records in his office and wrote them up about once a week; they were on lined cards with columns for receipts, issues and the balance.

   Lodge claimed to do a stocktake every month and to investigate any differences between the records and the actual amount on hand. He certainly walked round the warehouse, and he produced stock sheets ...

WB   But do we know whether they corresponded with the stock on hand?

MC   Short of attending a stocktake with him and checking all his figures, we couldn't tell.

WB   And we never did?

MC   We did ask on several occasions for a full stocktake when we were carrying out the 1987 audit. Lodge didn't want us to accompany him on the monthly stocktakes he did during the year. He said that it would have held him back too much if he had to explain everything as he went along. He could be very aggressive, and I suppose we didn't want to upset him at the start of our involvement with the company. If he had been unco-operative, it would have been disastrous, given that we were so heavily reliant on him for information and explanations in most of the audit areas.

WB   But you attended the year-end stocktake in 1987?

MC   One of our trainees attended part of it. It was very inconveniently timed. Lodge could manage to hold it only on Christmas Eve that year, because the company was going to close down until 6 January and Dickens needed to have figures on 3 January. Dickens agreed to the count being held on Christmas Eve because there weren't going to be any stock movements between then and the year-end. But Lodge started the count after lunch when most of our staff were off home for Christmas. I managed to find a junior trainee who lives locally who was prepared to attend.

WB   With any previous stocktaking experience?

MC   No, unfortunately. But he followed our standard procedures – made tests of some of Lodge's counts and took details of the stock sheets used. He found that the number of drums he counted agreed with Lodge's counts, and he had a few drums opened and ensured that they contained alloy and not scrap.

WB   What other audit work did we do on stock?

MC   This is a summary of the audit programme:

INTERIM TESTS

1. For a representative sample of 50 receipts per stock card:
   - check to delivery note and ensure details of quantity, type, etc. are in agreement;
   - agree price to supplier's invoice and check that total value on stock card has been correctly calculated.

2. For a representative sample of 50 issues from stock per stock card:
   - check to entry in duplicate book and ensure that details of quantity, type, etc. are in agreement;
   - ensure that amount issued has been deducted from the balance per the stock card.

3. For a representative sample of 50 stock cards, check accuracy of all additions and calculations.

4. Ensure that all journal adjustments to stock in excess of £25,000 have been authorized by Mr Lodge.

FINAL

1. Attend stocktake; perform test counts and complete report on attendance.

2. Check arithmetical accuracy of the stock sheets.

3. Trace totals from stock sheets to balance sheet.

4. Ensure that stocks are valued at invoice price on a FIFO basis, in accordance with company's policy.

5. Ensure by reference to current selling price list that stocks are valued at lower of cost and NRV.

6. Discuss with Mr Lodge the basis on which the obsolete stock provision has been calculated and ensure that it appears adequate.

WB   And this is the audit work you carried out on stocks in 1987 and 1988?

JL   Yes. Of course, we also included stocks in the company's and the group's letters of representation. Lodge signed the Brighter Alloys letter and Hart and the MD of Dickens signed for the group.

WB   Did you find any errors in your testing?

JL   No, nothing at all, really. The stock records seemed to be very accurately maintained and no errors emerged at the stocktake.

MC   I can see that Dickens are upset, but surely they can't blame us for the loss, can they? We tested the accuracy of the records and they looked all right. We attended the stocktake; we ensured stock was valued in accordance with SSAP 9. I admit we missed the fraud, but any approach based on sampling involves a risk that errors will be overlooked. The audit isn't a guarantee that no fraud has occurred.

QUESTIONS FOR DISCUSSION

1. Mark comments that 'any approach based on sampling involves a risk that errors will be overlooked. The audit isn't a guarantee that no fraud has occurred'. How far do his views reflect the spirit of the auditing guidelines?
2. What measures might have prevented or detected the fraud at Brighter Alloys, and whose responsibility were they?

Relevant reading

SAS 110: *Fraud and error*
(APC Auditing Guideline 418: *The auditor's responsibility in relation to fraud, other irregularities and errors*)

Case 15
Banbury Group plc

BACKGROUND

Banbury Group plc (B) was founded as a private company in 1959 and went public in 1964. Its main activities are the manufacture, sale and servicing of machinery for use in the food processing industry.

DOCUMENTS

15.1   Summarized accounts of Banbury Group plc 1994–1996

£000	1994	1995	1996
Turnover	27,849	41,508	39,320
Cost of sales	20,676	30,719	31,641
GROSS PROFIT	7,173	10,789	7,679
Selling and admin expenses	6,127	9,605	8,871
Other operating income	(256)	(138)	(347)
Redundancy costs	27	–	–
Reorganization and restructuring costs	484	141	2,176
Interest receivable	(27)	(54)	(104)
Interest payable	645	1,235	1,229
PROFIT/(LOSS) BEFORE TAX	173	–	(4,146)
Taxation	158	192	127
PROFIT/(LOSS) AFTER TAX	15	(192)	(4,273)
Minority interest	11	9	–
ATTRIBUTABLE TO MEMBERS	4	(201)	(4,273)
NOTES			
Interest payable			
Short term	402	842	943
Long term	54	165	78
Debenture	–	52	51
Lease and HP	–	–	29
Other	189	176	128
	645	1,235	1,229

Profit before tax is after charging/(crediting):

	1994	1995	1996
Asset disposal	20	–	–
Subsidiary disposal	–	–	(186)
Grants received	(32)	(15)	–
Depreciation	484	660	795
Plant hire	166	253	318
Auditors' remuneration	99	166	175
Directors' emoluments	134	241	348
Compensation for loss of office	–	105	–

CONSOLIDATED BALANCE SHEETS

	1994	1995	1996
FIXED ASSETS			
Tangible fixed assets	4,494	4,997	5,193
Investments	17	17	21
	4,511	5,014	5,214
CURRENT ASSETS			
Stocks	6,572	10,180	10,457
Trade debtors	6,163	8,099	9,850
Other debtors	200	625	746
Prepayments	280	453	651
Tax recoverable	247	150	112
Cash	420	891	1,138
	13,882	20,398	22,954
CREDITORS (due within 1 year)			
Bank loans and overdrafts	2,526	5,022	6,293
Loans	195	437	768
Trade creditors	3,854	6,016	6,214
Bills of exchange	754	802	941
Current tax	28	34	105
Other taxes and social security	798	740	1,052
Other creditors	1,640	887	1,547
Accruals	2,016	2,974	2,557
	11,811	16,912	19,477
Net current assets	2,071	3,486	3,477
TOTAL ASSETS LESS CURRENT LIABILITIES	6,582	8,500	8,691
CREDITORS (due after one year)			
Loans and debenture stock	1,375	2,715	3,222
Other creditors	275	353	662

PROVISIONS

Other provisions	–	–	1,484
Deferred taxation	197	203	296
	1,847	3,271	5,664
	4,735	5,229	3,027
Share capital	1,614	2,421	3,631
Share premium account	4,101	4,101	4,455
Merger reserve	–	597	699
Revaluation reserve	1,563	1,563	1,124
Profit and loss account	(2,562)	(3,503)	(6,901)
Minority interest	19	50	19
	4,735	5,229	3,027

SUMMARIZED CASH FLOW STATEMENTS

£000	1994	1995	1996
Cash flow from operating activities	921	799	(1,273)
Returns on investment and servicing finance	(618)	(1,181)	(1,125)
Taxation	(252)	(135)	101
Capital expenditure	(1,065)	(617)	(1,126)
Financing	385	(92)	2,068
Decrease in cash	(629)	(1,226)	(1,355)

15.2　Capital structure of Banbury Group plc

B's capital is made up of:

Ordinary shares of 10p	28,244,674	£2,824,467
Deferred ordinary shares of 10p	8,069,907	£806,991

15.3　Extract from permanent audit file: structure of Banbury Group plc

B is the parent company. The following are wholly-owned subsidiaries:

Banbury Processing Equipment Ltd (incorporated in the UK)
Banbury North American Inc. (incorporated in the USA)
Banbury France SA (incorporated in France)
Banbury BV (incorporated in the Netherlands)
Franklin Corporation Inc., incorporated in the USA, was acquired by B on 5 April 1995 and disposed of on 25 July 1997

15.4   Chairman's statement at the annual general meeting of Banbury Group plc, held on 11 July 1997

The AGM approved the accounts for the year ended 30 November 1996. The Chairman stated:

1996 was an exceptionally difficult year for the group. The group's results were seriously affected by the substantial losses incurred both by Banbury Processing Equipment and by Franklin Corporation. The proceeds of the rights issue were mainly absorbed in paying the creditors of Banbury Processing Equipment, and not, as had been hoped, in reducing borrowings in order to stabilize the group's financial position. Your board concluded that the continuing programme of disposing of peripheral business segments was not by itself adequate to ensure that the group would return to financial stability. It concluded that it would be necessary to dispose of some of the core businesses so that the resources generated by disposal could be directed to those activities with the best prospects for the future. The group has accordingly undertaken a review of its activities, on the basis of which it has taken a number of significant decisions. Banbury Processing Equipment is currently trading from two sites; the review we have undertaken suggests that this is not a viable basis for continuing operations. Accordingly, the company's plant at Reading is to be closed and the property disposed of during the current year.

The group has entered into a contract with Stellar Properties to dispose of the site for £750,000 cash. The activities of the restructured company will be focused on currently profitable products and on products which have the potential to be made profitable. The order book is currently healthy, and a new managing director has recently joined the company. In order to improve the company's liquidity, the freehold interest in the company's site at Portsmouth is to be sold to Prospero Securities Ltd for a consideration of £1,550,000. The sale is subject to a lease-back to Banbury Processing Equipment for twenty-five years at an initial rent of £220,000, to be reviewed every five years.

The total employee numbers of the restructured company have been reduced from 450 at the end of 1996 to 199. The company is still constrained by a shortage of cash, but there are already indications that the restructured Banbury Processing Equipment is well placed to contribute to the future profitability of the group.

The benefits which the group had expected to arise from the merger with Franklin Corporation have not materialized. The profits which were confidently forecast at the time of the merger have not been achieved; instead, Franklin has suffered a substantial loss. This has been the result of technical problems experienced with new products which have had an adverse effect on sales. The US market has also shown a downturn, reflecting increased European competition. We have, unfortunately, no reason to expect that conditions will improve in the foreseeable future. Your board has accordingly taken the decision, subject to the approval of shareholders, to sell Franklin to Peoria Inc., for a consideration of £1,350,000.

The board is happy to report that the group's European subsidiaries have enjoyed a successful year. Banbury BV, in particular, has continued to develop markets in Germany, where the new products it introduced late in 1996 were well received. Both Banbury SA and Banbury BV have strong order books for the current year.

The restructuring described above will have the effect of reducing the group's borrowings by £5,900,000. The board is happy to record the group's gratitude to its principal bankers for their continuing support. In the UK, where cash constraints have been particularly acute, Barlloyds Bank has renewed the group's facility on normal terms, including the right to require repayment on demand, subject to the implementation of the restructuring programme and the continuing recovery of the group's financial position.

The group's trading loss and the provisions made for restructuring its operations have significantly eroded its reserves. As a result, the group has exceeded the borrowing limits imposed by its articles of association and by the 9 per cent Debenture Stock 1999–2006 Trust Deed. It is accordingly proposed that the group's borrowing limit be increased from one and one half to three and one half times its share capital and consolidated reserves. The trustee under the debenture stock deed has agreed to amend the trust deed, subject to an increase in the interest rate of the stock to 13 per cent with immediate effect.

[*Note*: The AGM ratified all the proposals contained in the Chairman's report.]

15.5   Interim report of Banbury Group plc for the half-year to 31 May 1997, issued 5 November 1997

(Comparative figures show six months ending 31 May 1996.)

£000	1997	1996
Sales	11,605	19,387
Operating costs	11,700	18,836
Loss on disposal of Franklin Corporation	436	–
Interest payable	490	632
Loss before taxation	1,021	81
Taxation	36	103
Minority interest	–	2
Operating loss	1,057	186

The board wishes to report that the operating result was in line with expectations, although slightly affected by production delays at Portsmouth. It appears likely, however, that the shortfall will be made up by the end of the year. The asset disposal programme outlined in the Chairman's statement in August 1996 has been completed and the rationalization plan is being implemented. Interest charges for the first half-year have fallen substantially as a result of the disposal of Franklin Corporation and it is expected that the major reduction in borrowings in the UK will be reflected in a further interest reduction in the second half-year.

The continental subsidiaries continue to show satisfactory performance. Banbury BV is extending its factory in order to meet increasing demand for its products while reducing lead time for meeting orders. Banbury SA has experienced some production problems, but has launched a successful new product which is currently creating considerable interest. Banbury Processing Equipment continues to be the principal area of concern. Your board anticipates a gradual but steady improvement in the performance of the company rather than a spectacular recovery.

The group's net assets have now fallen below half the nominal value of its issued share capital. An Extraordinary General Meeting has been convened for 26 November to decide how the situation is to be dealt with.

15.6　Announcements by the board of Banbury Group plc

26 November 1997 At the Extraordinary General Meeting of Banbury Group plc held today, the Chairman stated that the board's initial intention, as outlined in its interim report, had been to continue with the restructuring plan approved at the AGM. It had become apparent, however, that the group would require further resources in order to carry out the planned restructuring. The group's strategy for obtaining additional finance was under discussion and a decision was to be expected in the next few weeks.

11 December 1997 The board is considering an approach made to it by Mr R. N. Bennett, Chief Executive of the group. This may result in an offer being made to buy its share capital. Various other third parties have expressed an interest in the group as a whole or in certain of its activities.

20 January 1998 At the request of the group, listing for its shares has been temporarily suspended with effect from 1.00 p.m. today.

13 February 1998 Following a deterioration in the group's financial position, the directors announce that the approach made by Mr R. N. Bennett has now been withdrawn. No progress has been made in discussions with the other parties who expressed an interest in the group. In the absence of additional finance, the directors of Banbury Processing Equipment have decided that the company could not properly continue to trade. Barlloyds Bank was accordingly invited to appoint a receiver, and Messrs B. Smith and L. Simms of Parker and Simms were appointed joint administrative receivers of the company on 12 February 1998.

11 January 1999 At the request of the group, the listing for its securities suspended on 20 January 1998 has been cancelled with effect from 9.00 a.m. today.

QUESTIONS FOR DISCUSSION

The audit report on the Banbury Group's financial statements for the year ended 30 November 1996 was signed on 30 June 1997.

1. What aspects of the Banbury Group's results in 1996 might have given the auditor cause for concern? What work should the auditor have done in view of the circumstances of the Banbury Group?
2. On the basis of the evidence available to the auditor at the date when the audit report was signed, how should the audit report have been worded?

Relevant reading

APB SAS 130: *The going concern basis in financial statements*
APB SAS 600: *Auditors' reports on financial statements*

Case 16
Sunrise Holdings plc

BACKGROUND

Sunrise Holdings plc was formed in 1980 by Ted Stainer. The group has expanded through acquisitions of chains of shops, including women's and children's clothes shops. In July 1994, Sunrise acquired Glamour Ltd, a private company which owned four shops selling jewellery and fashion accessories. Sunrise purchased 100 per cent of the issued share capital of Glamour for £700,000 from the company's five shareholders, all members of the Marsh family who had set up and run the business.

Small & Partners had been Glamour Ltd's auditors since the company was formed in 1989. They issued an unqualified audit opinion on Glamour's 1994 accounts in May 1994.

DOCUMENTS

16.1   Letter from Ted Stainer to Small & Partners, 21 April 1994

> Sunrise plc
> Sunrise House
> Gritborough

Small & Partners
Commercial Chambers
Clagthorpe

Dear Sirs

We understand that you are the auditors of Glamour Ltd. The Sunrise Group is currently contemplating the acquisition of the share capital of Glamour Ltd. We shall, in deciding whether to proceed with the acquisition, place reliance on the audited financial statements of Glamour Ltd for the year ended 31 March 1994.

Yours faithfully

E. Stainer

(Small & Partners did not reply to this letter)

16.2   Summarized accounts of Glamour Ltd for the year ended 31 March 1994

	£000
Fixed assets	350
Current assets	
Stock	295
Debtors and prepayments	35
Cash and bank	22
	352
Current liabilities	
Creditors and accruals	141
Net assets	561
Shareholders' funds	
Share capital	380
Retained profits	181
	561

	£000
Turnover	1,000
Cost of sales	700
Gross profit	300
Expenses	220
Net profit	80

Following the acquisition, Sunrise carried out a detailed investigation of Glamour Ltd, and drew up a revised set of accounts.

	£000
Fixed assets	350
Current assets	
Stock	180
Debtors and prepayments	29
Cash and bank	22
	231
Current liabilities	
Creditors and accruals	160
Net assets	421

Shareholders' funds

Share capital	380
Retained profits	41
	421

	£000
Turnover	1,000
Cost of sales	760
Gross profit	240
Expenses	245
Net loss	(5)

Restatement of retained profits:

	£000
Per audited accounts	181
Revision of result for 1994	(85)
Prior year adjustment	(55)
As restated	41

The restatement of the financial statements was found necessary for the following reasons:

Stock: It was discovered that there had been a fraud at Glamour's largest branch. The shop manager, who was responsible for stocktaking, had been stealing jewellery to sell in her own business, and systematically falsifying stock returns. When a full count was carried out by Sunrise, stock losses of £40,000 were found, going back over 2 years. It was also found that provisions for slow-moving and obsolete stock at all branches were inadequate. As a result, 1994 opening and closing stock figures were heavily written down.

Debtors and prepayments: These were found to have been overstated as a result of a computer programming error which had caused certain utilities prepayments to be doubled.

Creditors and accruals: Because of errors in the year-end cut-off procedures, goods received and not invoiced by suppliers had been overlooked, resulting in an understatement of accruals.

16.3 Memorandum from Ted Stainer to the directors of Sunrise Holdings plc 1 December 1995

As you are all aware, recent events have revealed that serious financial irregularities had occurred at Glamour Ltd in the period before that company was acquired by our group. The paper attached to this memorandum sets out the nature of these irregularities. It is apparent that:

- *Management controls over Glamour's assets and accounting system were inadequate, resulting in major fraud and the misstatement of assets and liabilities.*
- *The financial statements which were presented to this board when it was contemplating the acquisition of Glamour were seriously misleading. If the true financial position of Glamour had been stated, this group would not have proceeded with the acquisition.*

In my opinion, the responsibility for the misleading information presented to this board lies with Small & Partners, as auditors of Glamour Ltd. They were aware that it was our intention to acquire that company, and that we were relying on the financial statements for the year ending 31 December 1994 in making our decision. We consider that they gave an unqualified audit opinion negligently.

Accordingly, I wish to convene a meeting of this board at 9.00 a.m. on 4 December to discuss the steps that should be taken to recover damages from Small & Partners in respect of the loss suffered by this group in acquiring Glamour Ltd.

16.4   Article in *Accountancy News* week ending 8 December 1995

WE'RE NOT WORRIED CLAIMS GLAMOUR AUDIT PARTNER

Terry Small, interviewed yesterday by *Accountancy News*, was apparently unworried by the announcement that Sunrise plc intends to sue Small & Partners for the losses the group claims to have incurred as a result of acquiring the troubled Glamour jewellery chain last year.

'Sunrise have changed their minds about Glamour', Small asserted, 'and now the board is trying to use us as a scapegoat. My partners and I are determined to resist their claim in the courts. In the first place, a large part of the restatement of Glamour's figures is judgmental, based on a different assessment of stock values. Stock in the fashion business is subject to fluctuations as consumer tastes alter; everybody knows that accounting is based on estimates. We refuse to be blamed because an accounting estimate needed revision.'

Secondly, Small insists that his firm did not have any duties towards Sunrise. 'The shareholders of Glamour were paying our fees; we wrote an audit report addressed to them, not to anybody who might come along and take an interest in the company. If Sunrise wanted information to help them decide about the acquisition, it was up to them to commission a special report. Financial accounts are a historical document, not a prediction of future performance. Anybody who buys a company on the basis of its last year's accounts and nothing else wants his head looking at.'

According to Small, it would be 'a disaster for the auditing profession' if Sunrise were to succeed in its claim. 'Auditors would be constantly looking over their shoulders in case anybody wanted to rely on accounts for any purpose, however unreasonable that reliance might be. That would drive up the costs of auditing, to the detriment of everybody, not least the shareholders and public at large who would pay those costs through higher prices. Firms like ours would be driven out of auditing completely'.

Ted Stainer was unrepentant in responding to Small's comments. 'If you take Small's attitude to its logical conclusion, the audit is worthless – it doesn't give assurance to anybody, and we might as well get rid of the whole charade. Auditors can't have it both ways. If the audit report is worth paying for, it must mean something, and surely it must mean the same to everybody who reads it, whether they're shareholders or not! Either accounts give a fair picture of a company's performance or they don't. Auditors should admit their responsibility to everybody who uses accounts'.

QUESTIONS FOR DISCUSSION

1. Analyse the reasons for the difference between the audited 1994 result of Glamour and the revised result calculated by Sunrise. How far do you agree with Small's comment that it is based on differences in accounting estimates?
2. Evaluate the arguments put forward by Ted Stainer and Terry Small about the extent of Small's liability to Sunrise plc.
3. Comment on the remarks made by Ted Stainer and Terry Small in Document 16.4 about the desirability or otherwise of making auditors liable to users of accounts other than shareholders. Does auditor liability serve a useful function?

Relevant reading

APC Practice Note 4: *Reliance by banks on audited financial statements*
Gwilliam, D. (1988) Does care extend beyond the contract?, *Accountancy*, May, pp. 17–18
Institute of Chartered Accountants in England and Wales (1995) Managing the professional liability of accountants, *Members' Handbook*, ICAEWA, London
Mills, C. (1990) *The Caparo Decision*, Coopers & Lybrand Deloitte
Pearse, C. (1994) Love thy Neighbour? *Accountancy*, November, pp. 160–1

Case 17
The European Hotels Group plc

BACKGROUND

The European Hotels Group plc (EHG) was founded in 1973 by Thomas Green. At its inception, the company owned one country house hotel in Sussex. It grew by acquisitions to become one of the largest hotel businesses in the UK before trading in its shares was suspended in 1994.

DOCUMENTS

17.1   Chronology of EHG

1973   Thomas Green purchases 100 per cent shareholding in the Thatchers Arms, Arundel.

1983   Changes company's name to European Hotels Group. £30m rights issue. Buys 17 hotels from Acme Leisure UK for £20m.

1984   Second rights issue for £12m.

1987   Third rights issue for £22m. Buys Dutch Kurhaus Hotels for £15m.

1988   Fourth rights issue for £70m. Buys 12 hotels in Belgium and 5 in France from Groupe Loisirs for £100m.

1990   Fifth rights issue for £55m. Takes over Scottish Hostelries plc for £114m.

May 1992   £180m rights issue. Pays £50m for 19 European hotels.

June 1992   Issues £180m redeemable preference shares.

December 1993   Interim results of group reveal net debt of £800m.

March 1994   Trading in shares suspended.

17.2   Share price of EHG (in pence)

1983	20
1984	20
1985	37
1986	33
1987	42
1988	80
1989	75
1990	110
1991	100
1992	105
1993	90
1994	40

17.3   Extract from the *City Chronicle*, 30 June 1994

OUTCRY IN CITY OVER EHG DEBACLE

Shareholders and analysts expressed 'anger and astonishment' yesterday after the release of the 1993/4 results of the ailing hotel chain EHG. Fears for its future were aroused as early as last December by the disclosure of an unprecedented level of indebtedness. Shortly after trading in its shares was suspended in March this year, there was a wave of resignations among the executive team. Guy Wills and Tim Parker, respectively deputy chairman and finance director, quit the company in April, and Tom Green, the hard-driving entrepreneur who founded EHG in 1973, resigned as chairman in June. His replacement, Richard Baxter, yesterday had the unhappy task of announcing that EHG's asset base has disappeared. The group's results show a deficit of £1000m, due mainly to a write-down of £850m of its properties. The 1994 valuation of EHG's hotels carried out by surveyors Patterdale & Glen on Baxter's instructions was nearly £900m lower than the previous valuation performed in 1992 by Nesbitt & Buxton. Representatives of the two firms of surveyors yesterday defended their respective positions. A Nesbitt spokesman described the recent valuations as 'exaggeratedly conservative'. Patterdale senior partner Dominic Bland pointed out that pessimism about EHG's trading future would necessarily affect the values placed on its properties.

There was more bad news. Baxter, who engaged chartered accountants Forsyte & Fawcett to investigate the group's financial position, reported that EHG may have paid dividends 'unlawfully' in its last 3 years of trading. Investors were yesterday par-ticularly resentful at the news that the group's directors had enjoyed pension arrangements which were never revealed to shareholders. All executive directors were paid a pension of two-thirds of final salary, regardless of the length of their service with EHG, a privilege that cost the group £5m annually. Forsyte & Fawcett are also understood to have been severely critical of EHG's accounting systems. Management information was minimal, and the group's treasury function was weak. EHG's auditors were Seldon & Co, 'a surprisingly small firm' as one analyst commented yesterday; Baxter is making it a priority to replace them with a 'big six' firm and strengthen accounting discipline in the group.

Adjustments behind record EHG loss

The main element in the group's huge 1994 loss was the massive property write down caused by the latest revaluation. But there were also significant restatements of the 1993 result which converted the original result – a profit of £90m – to a loss of £55m. These included £40m of depreciation – under Green, the group had not depreciated its hotels because of his contention that they were appreciating assets – and a £10m write-off of maintenance expenditure which had previously been capitalized. Overstated profits on the sale of fixed assets, overstated income from an incentive scheme, and other capitalized expenses made up the remainder of the write-down. The 1993 interim figures could not be restated, explained Baxter, because the working papers on which they were based were 'missing' from the group's headquarters.

17.4   Extract from the *Sunday Clarion*, 3 July 1994

EHG: WHAT WENT WRONG?

The Sunday Clarion City team look at the background to the hotel chain's startling collapse. EHG started small, as a sideline for Thomas Green, partner in a Sussex firm of estate agents, when in 1973 he took over a local country hotel. Green's success in converting the run-down premises into a conference venue and health club persuaded him to branch out. Ten years later, with bank finance, he acquired the sound but underperforming Acme Leisure Group and founded his European hotel empire.

Green's management style changed little over the next decade. Its hallmarks were close personal involvement by Green in the day to day running of the group and what he described as a 'lean' head office. In a 1989 interview with the *Sunday Clarion*, Green expressed his distaste for 'delegation and bureaucracy'. He went on to expound his management philosophy; 'EHG has grown through seizing opportunities and taking chances. I don't want to hamper it with a bureaucratic apparatus that means every decision has to be approved three or four times before anything happens. I think the results vindicate my approach.' Certainly in the 1980s EHG posted impressive results. Green took the business into Europe, and found no difficulty in going back to the City repeatedly for finance. EHG's track record was the envy of its hotel industry competitors; Green was widely admired for his tireless pursuit of profit growth through acquisitions.

But institutional investors also raised their eyebrows at the way the company was run. There was little formal management information, and the 'lean' head office did not have a treasury function despite its large foreign exchange exposure. Green's entrepreneurial talent was recognized and respected, but there were fears that he did not have a sufficiently strong team backing him up. Seldon, the small audit firm who had been with Green from the outset, had little to say about the absence of a sophisticated accounting system. Main board directors were issued with monthly summaries of 'key' data, but required to hand them back at the end of each board meeting; Green was the only one with his finger on the pulse. It became harder to monitor performance as the group continued to expand and its position became more complex.

The final crisis came in March this year. EHG was renegotiating its borrowing with the banks; debt had increased dramatically because of the fall of sterling against the D-Mark. The group was attempting to boost reported profits and please its bankers by operating an elaborate incentive scheme which involved booking income from room sales for the following 12 months on the first day of the accounting period. It was also entering into a series of sale and leaseback property deals designed to cut debt. Despite the uncertainties, management was confident that it would achieve the £80m profit forecast on which the refinancing depended. But when the returns from EHG's continental divisions were consolidated with the UK results, the group profit was £20m short of the forecast. Directors – including Green

– and advisers were 'shocked'; the chain of events that ended in Green's departure had begun.

Whose fault was the collapse of EHG? Unsurprisingly, there is no consensus about the culprits. Many blame Green for his bullish management style, and believe that he fatally overestimated his ability to manage a large, complex group with minimal controls. Green himself rejects claims that his approach was at fault. He blames adverse trading conditions. 'There is always an element of luck in business, and we ran out of luck. I'm desperately sad and disappointed for everybody who's been hurt by this, but these things happen. I still believe EHG has a lot of potential'.

'Hurt' investors blame Green, but also the group's advisers; in particular the auditors, Seldon, who are criticized as ineffectual and afraid of standing up to Green. There are also harsh words for the group's non-executive directors. One analyst was scathing: 'These guys did nothing for their fees. They tolerated shambolic systems, minimal information, being harangued by Green at every board meeting – and they said nothing. What point is there in having non-execs when somebody like Green can walk all over them?' The non-executives deny that they were negligent or weak. They claim that they asked questions about the group's performance and prospects, but that the answers they received from Green and his executive board members were evasive or misleading. They 'had no idea' of the controversial pension enhancement package from which executives benefited.

But shouldn't all sides have been warier? With hindsight, there were plenty of danger signals before the final collapse. The last word is with an investment analyst who admits advising his clients to invest in EHG. 'In the end, you have to trust somebody. We trusted Green and his board. They took responsibility for those accounts. Okay, the figures were too good to be true, but we had an auditor's report to say that they were true. What were we supposed to do – ask to see the management accounts?'

QUESTIONS FOR DISCUSSION

1. What were the 'danger signals' that the *Sunday Clarion* mentions?
2. How far could it be argued that the collapse of EHG represents an audit failure?
3. What elements of corporate governance in the UK, apart from audit, might be implicated in the collapse of EHG?

Relevant reading

APB Bulletin 1995/1: *Disclosures relating to corporate governance*
Cadbury Committee (1992) *Report of the Committee on the Financial Aspects of Corporate Governance* Gee & Co, London
SAS 300: *Accounting and internal controls and audit risk assessments*
(APC Auditing Standard 204: *Internal controls*)
SAS 520: *Using the work of an expert*
(APC Auditing Standard 413: *Reliance on other specialists*)

Case 18
Homejoy Products Limited

BACKGROUND

Homejoy Products is the UK subsidiary of the European Schoenheim Group, whose headquarters are in Frankfurt. Homejoy's UK sites and operations are summarized below:

Bletchley factory employing 600 people. Manufactures washing-up liquid and household cleaners which are sold via shops and supermarkets under the Homejoy brand and as supermarket own-brand products. Sales of products manufactured in Bletchley in 1994 accounted for 55 per cent of Homejoy's turnover – £6.6m.

Cambridge factory employing 250 people. Manufactures detergents and dishwasher powder, both under the Homejoy brand and as supermarket own-brands. Sales of Cambridge products were £3.6m in 1994.

Dundee factory employing 100 people. Manufactures industrial cleaning agents and solvents which are sold direct to end-users. Sales were £1.8m in 1994.

Evesham distribution depot employing 35 people. The company's fleet of 15 lorries, used for distributing products to customers, operates from here, and the site also contains the distribution warehouse.

Faversham, Homejoy's head office, employing 120 people.

PEOPLE INVOLVED

Frankfurt
Erich Kloss: Group Chief Executive.

Faversham
William Wright: Managing Director, UK operations.
Albert Holt: Finance Director.
Sarah Liu: Internal Audit Manager.

DOCUMENTS

18.1   Memo from Erich Kloss to William Wright

Frankfurt
19 July 1995

Environmental audit
As you will no doubt be aware, the Schoenheim Group attaches the utmost importance to environmental protection. That is why I am writing to the

managing directors of all our divisions on the important issue of environmental audit. With effect from 1 July 1996, all divisions will be required to
perform a regular environmental audit and report the outcome to group
headquarters.

The board of directors recognizes that there are differences between legal
regimes in the various European states in which the Schoenheim group
operates, and also that the different businesses in which we are active will
have different environmental implications. We therefore do not intend to
prescribe immediately an environmental audit approach to be implemented
by all group companies. Instead, in the short term, we are inviting divisions
to draw up their own plans for an environmental audit. Our only stipulation
is that the exercise should comply with the definition of environmental audit
set out by the International Chamber of Commerce in 1988:

'A management tool comprising a systematic, documented, periodic
and objective evaluation of how well environmental organization,
management and equipment are performing with the aim of helping
to safeguard the environment by (i) facilitating management control
of environmental practices; and (ii) assessing compliance with
company policies, which would include meeting regulatory
requirements'.

I look forward to receiving from you by 31 December 1995 an outline of your
company's environmental audit plan for 1996.

E. Kloss

18.2   Memo from William Wright to Albert Holt

Faversham 28 July 1995

*Al – I just got this from Frankfurt. What do they want now? Let me know
what we'll need to do to keep them quiet and what it'll cost.*

18.3 Memo from Albert Holt to William Wright

Faversham 4 August 1995

*Bill – I don't know exactly what we'll have to do, but I've spoken to the auditors,
and they say there are no laws about this kind of thing in the UK. Apparently
we can do it all ourselves if we want to – we don't have to pay for an
independent audit. Of course they said their management consultancy division
could do us an audit if we wanted, but if we don't have to pay for it I don't see
why we should. This is the kind of one-off exercise that's a natural for internal
audit. Sarah comes from a top-class accountancy firm and she's got loads of
common sense. I'm sure she'll be able to cope with it. We can always borrow one
of the engineers to help her out for a few days when she's doing tests.*

*As far as the actual audit work is concerned, I think it's going to be
essentially the same as the systems testing Sarah normally does – like the*

in-depth investigation of the Purchasing Department she carried out last year. We have various systems generating evidence relating to environmental matters, for instance:

- *records of regulations and permits granted;*
- *monitoring data for emissions to air and water;*
- *records of our waste disposal arrangements;*
- *emergency and disaster plans;*
- *standing instructions on health and safety;*
- *incident records for accidents on-site;*
- *minutes of the factory health and safety committees*

and all of these could be the subject of tests. As I see it, the main purpose of the audit is to make sure we're approaching things in a systematic way and complying with the law – not so different from the financial audit.

18.4 Memo from Albert Holt to Sarah Liu

Faversham 4 August 1995

Sarah – I need some ideas from you about the way we might put together an environmental audit. There don't seem to be any professional guidelines, but you might use the attached as a starting-point; it's to do with some EC proposals. Have a look at that and anything else you can find, and then let me have your suggestions about the following:

1. *Which sites ought we to cover? Should we just look at Bletchley or should we do all the factories? Presumably we needn't cover Evesham and Faversham.*

2. *What tests should we carry out? Possible ones that occur to me include:*

   - *review of emissions data month by month to make sure they're within the consented limits;*
   - *review of monthly data about time lost due to accidents etc;*
   - *check that safety inspections are carried out in accordance with schedule;*
   - *check that the documentation relating to waste disposal is in order.*

3. *What staff should be involved and when?*

4. *What kind of audit report should be produced? Something along the lines of 'The environmental performance of Homejoy Ltd for the year ended 30 June 1996 has been satisfactory' is what I have in mind, but feel free to make your own suggestions.*

Anyway, over to you.

18.5   Attached to Albert Holt's memo: Extract from *EC Eco-Management and Audit Scheme: an introductory guide for industry (UK Department of the Environment, 1995)*

A step-by-step guide
In order to participate in EMAS, you will be required to implement each of the following at the relevant site:

1. Environmental policy
There must be a company-wide environmental policy before any individual site can be registered. This policy is the key tool to communicate the environmental priorities of your management and staff to the general public and other stakeholders.

It should have two central elements:
• compliance with relevant environmental regulations.
• a commitment to continuous improvement.

The policy should be written, and adopted, at the highest managerial level. To be truly effective, the policy should regularly be reviewed and revised – for example, after company audits. This will ensure that it is seen to be relevant, and a sign that your organization is striving for excellence.

2. Environmental review
This should be comprehensive analysis of the inputs, processes and outputs at the site to identify the relevant environmental impacts and issues for your management. Areas covered will include energy management, raw materials management, waste avoidance, evaluation of noise control, and current accident procedures. You will also need to list all the environmental legislation which applies to the site, and whether all of it is being observed.

3. Environmental programme
This should be set out in accordance with the policy and review. The programme should contain specific goals for the site, and describe the means to reach these objectives.

4. Environmental management system
You will need to establish operating procedures and controls to ensure the successful implementation of the environmental policy and programme. This will have implications for both your organizational structure and your people. For example, it may be necessary to appoint environmental managers or to change job descriptions and performance criteria to reflect new responsibilities. You may choose to devise your own management system or use a recognized standard such as BS 7750.

5. Environmental audit cycle
This is the process whereby your environmental practices and performances are checked against your stated policy, specific goals, and relevant regulations and standards. Internal audits are, of course, a normal feature of good management systems and are a requirement under EMAS and BS 7750. Periodic audits give

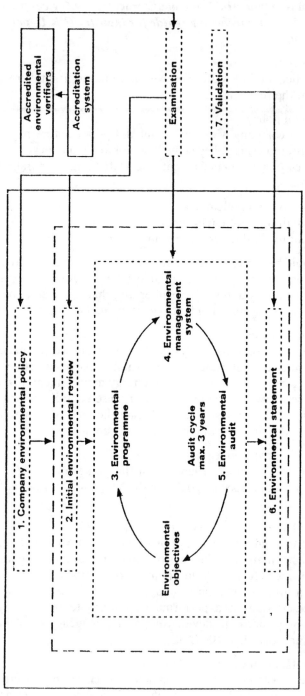

Source of diagram: 'EMAS: A Practical Guide'. ISBN: 0-946655-81-2.

you the necessary information to exercise control over management practices and the development of specific improvements. The frequency of the full audit cycle will depend upon the nature and risks associated with activities on the site, but must take place at least every three years.

The initial registration of a site may be based on information gathered in the environmental review, provided that the environmental management system is fully operational. Audit programmes need not be completed prior to the first registration, but you should still describe the audit process, as this must be carried out in the first and subsequent cycles.

6. Environmental statement

After the initial review and, generally, each subsequent year, you will be required to prepare a concise and comprehensible statement for the public, for each participating site. The purpose of the statement is to ensure that the public, and all interested parties, understand the environmental impacts of the site, and how they are being managed. It should contain up-to-date information on progress against the objectives and time scales agreed by the site's management team.

7. Validation

The environmental statement must be verified by an independent accredited environmental verifier at the end of each cycle. The policy, programme, management system and audit procedure also have to be validated. However, if the systems on the site are certified to BS 7750, they will already meet the corresponding EMAS requirements. The government is seeking official recognition from the European Commission, which will make this completely automatic.

18.6   Memo from Sarah Liu to Albert Holt

Faversham 29 August 1995

Albert – sorry for the delay in replying to your memo. I've been doing some reading about environmental audit, and I think there are some important issues we need to resolve before we go any further with planning our own exercise . . .

QUESTIONS FOR DISCUSSION

1. Comment on Albert's proposals for environmental audit. What are the advantages and limitations of his approach?
2. What do you think are the 'important issues' that Sarah wants to resolve? What solutions would you propose?

Relevant reading

Elkington, J. (1990) *The Environmental Audit, a green filter for company policies, plants, processes and products*, SustainAbility, London

Gray, R., Bebbington, J. and Walters, D. (1993) *Accounting for the Environment*, ACCA/Paul Chapman Publishing, London

International Chamber of Commerce (1991) *An ICC Guide to Effective Environmental Auditing*, ICC Publishing, SA Paris

Owen, D. (ed.) (1992) *Green Reporting: Accountancy and the challenge of the nineties*, Chapman & Hall, London

Wheatley, M. (1993) *Green Business*, Institute of Management/Pitman Publishing, London

Case 19
Pen & Paper plc

BACKGROUND

Tick & Co. are auditors of Pen & Paper plc (P&P), a chain of 32 stationery shops located throughout the UK, and is currently planning the 19X7 audit. The management of P&P has made it clear that it expects the audit fee to be lower than it was in 19X6, and the audit partner and manager are currently planning the audit work with a view to meeting the client's expectations while obtaining adequate audit assurance.

PEOPLE INVOLVED

Tick & Co.
Sarah Miller: audit partner.
James Denham: audit manager.

Pen & Paper plc
Norman Wright: finance director.
Ellen Lawson: internal audit manager.
Steven Broom: internal audit assistant.

DOCUMENTS

19.1   Extract from Tick & Co's permanent audit file notes on Pen & Paper plc (updated August 19X7)

Nature of the business

P&P was formed in 19X0 as a private company, running 2 shops in central London. Twelve more shops were opened over the following 5 years, mainly in the South-East. The company then expanded dramatically with the acquisition of Mackenzie & Co. (8 shops in Scotland) in 19X6 and D. Davies Ltd (10 shops in Wales and the West Midlands) this year.

The shops sell a wide range of stationery for home and business use; some of the stock reflects local demand, e.g. postcards and souvenirs in holiday resorts, artists' and technical drawing supplies at branches near colleges/ universities. This year, on a trial basis, the 5 largest branches began to sell a restricted range of computers and printers, and these items may be introduced to other branches if the results are good.

Results

Trading results for the past 2 years are summarized below, together with the projected result for 19X7.

(£000s)	19X5 (actual)	19X6 (actual)	19X7 (budget)
Turnover	4,200	6,820	10,240
Cost of sales	2,898	4,774	6,861
Gross profit	1,302	2,046	3,379
Operating expenses	1,224	1,964	3,176
Net profit	78	82	203

Accounting systems

This is an outline only; detailed notes are given in section B of the permanent file. (*Not included.*)

Bank and cash

Each shop has an electronic till which produces an audit roll listing all transactions. Every week, the till roll is sent to P&P's accounts department at head office in London, together with a sheet completed by the shop manager which summarizes cash takings and bankings on a daily basis and reconciles these with opening and closing cash in the till. Each branch has an account with the local branch of Midlays Bank; surplus cash is regularly transferred to the group's main account.

Purchases and stock

The majority of payments are transacted by head office – stock purchases, payroll, fixed assets, major repairs etc. Shop managers have a cheque authorization limit of £150, for expenditure on a fairly restricted range of items such as casual labour and minor repairs. Information about expenditure by shop managers is also reported to head office weekly.

Most of the stock is held centrally at the company's warehouse in Milton Keynes. Shop managers send a weekly order to Milton Keynes which is delivered by van. Some items are delivered direct to the shop by the supplier. Shop managers are required to perform a stock count every 4 weeks and return the results to head office. A team of stocktakers visits all shops on a rotating basis at least twice a year, and any differences between the stocktake results and the manager's return are investigated. The pattern of stocktake visits is planned to ensure that the branches with the highest stock value are checked close to the year-end (31 December).

Management information

The financial year is divided into 13 four-weekly accounting periods. For each period, management receives a trading account and details of key indicators – sales, gross and net profit and stock turnover – for each shop. Shop managers are provided with a four-weekly trading account for their shop.

Internal audit

An internal audit department was set up on 1 March 19X7, consisting of an audit manager and an assistant and reporting to the finance director. Its function is to carry out a regular programme of reviewing activities at shops, together with special one-off investigations on problem areas. At present, it is engaged on a review of cash handling procedures at shops.

19.2   Letter from Norman Wright to Sarah Miller, 31 August 19X7

Dear Sarah

I feel I must write to you to express my concern at the level of audit fee you are proposing this year. I see that you are suggesting a 7 per cent increase on last year's fee. I recognize that your staff costs have increased, and I note your assurance that the proposed fee does not fully reflect this increase. But I must remind you that our staff costs have increased appreciably as well – I mean by the establishment of an internal audit department. The total cost of employing Ellen and Steven is of the order of £50K per annum. I would expect this to have a substantial impact on the audit fee, given that they will, in effect, be doing the work that in previous years was carried out by your good selves.

   I have asked Ellen to arrange a meeting with James so that she can explain to him the nature of the audit work she has been doing. I hope that when that has been taken into account, you will be able to make a fee proposal that is more acceptable to us, and reflects the extra costs we are incurring.

Yours ever

Norman

19.3   Memo from James Denham to Sarah Miller

5 September 19X7

I have just got back from a meeting at Pen & Pencil to discuss the work being done by internal audit. I'll let you have a note of what was said as soon as possible, but basically I think it is good news. Internal audit has dealt with 3 major areas of the accounts – fixed assets, bank/cash and stock – and this presumably means that we can cut down our own work drastically, with implications for cost savings.

19.4   Note of a meeting held at the head office of Pen & Paper plc on 5 September 19X7

Present:

James Denham (JD)

Ellen Lawson (EL)

JD opened the meeting by explaining that he and the Tick & Co audit team wanted to gain an understanding of the work being done by the internal audit department. This would have an impact on the nature and amount of audit work they did.

EL explained that she had started work for Pen & Paper in March. Prior to that, she had worked for a large accountancy practice and qualified as a chartered accountant in December 19X6. Steven Broom, her assistant, had joined immediately after leaving school in July. They shared an office on the third floor of the company's headquarters, adjacent to that of Norman Wright, to whom they reported directly.

Mr Wright had set out a programme of work to be completed by the internal audit department. For the period April to December X7, it comprised:

1. A review of stocktaking procedures at branches to determine whether the costs of stocktaking could be reduced (completed July 19X7).
2. An in-depth check on cash and bank records at 3 large branches – Holborn, Edinburgh and Hull (covering April–August 19X7).
3. A review of the company's fixed asset records, involving a detailed census of the fixed assets held at each branch, with a view to accumulating data for a computerized fixed asset register (data to be collected by December 19X7).
4. An investigation of the possibilities for reducing energy consumption and increasing recycling of paper and other consumables at head office (to be completed by December X7).

The first 2 assignments had been completed on schedule. Detailed recommendations about reduction in staffing and frequency of stocktaking had been made and were being reviewed by Mr Wright. The results of the cash and bank review were satisfactory. EL offered to let JD have a copy of the reports. It seemed likely that the other work would also be finished in good time for the year-end audit visit, and again EL was sure it would be acceptable for the auditors to look at the reports sent to Mr Wright.

19.5   Memo from Sarah Miller to James Denham

6 September 19X7

Sorry, Jim, but I think you're jumping the gun. We need more information about the internal audit department before we decide how to use them. I suspect that, this year, we won't be able to make much of a dent in our costs by relying on them – but there is some scope for making use of their work.

QUESTIONS FOR DISCUSSION

1. What information do Tick & Co. need before they decide how to use the internal audit department? What are the underlying principles they need to bear in mind? What problems, if any, do you foresee?
2. How useful is the work of the internal audit department likely to be to the external auditors this year? How might it be made more useful?
3. Comment on Norman Wright's assertion that the internal audit department will in future do work previously done by the external auditors.

Relevant reading

SAS 500: *Considering the work of internal audit*
(APC 408: *Reliance on internal audit*)

Case 20
Finch & Co

BACKGROUND

Finch & Co. is a six-partner firm of chartered accountants, with an office in the small town of Bulhampton. Since the firm was founded in 1950, it has provided audit, tax and accountancy services to local private companies. The gross fee income of the partnership in 1994 was £450,000. The partners of Finch & Co. currently (May 1995) anticipate a visit from the Joint Monitoring Unit. Mike Dunn, who was made a partner in January, has been asked to review the firm's activities in order to identify any issues that might attract comment from the JMU.

PEOPLE INVOLVED

Partners in Finch & Co.
James Finch (JF) Senior Partner.
Glenn Warren. (GW)
Tom Craddock. (TC)
Sally Barnes. (SB)
Bill Lee. (BL)
Mike Dunn. (MD)

20.1 Memorandum from Mike Dunn to James Finch

James

My review of the audit files for the partnership suggests that there are a number of clients in respect of whom we may have some problems with the JMU. I have passed you the relevant files. Briefly, the clients in question are:

1.   Bladon Ltd (partner responsible GW)
According to our records, the following invoices are still outstanding for payment by Bladon:
Inv. no 93/202 dated 30 September 1993, for £12,000, being the balance of the 1993 audit fee
Inv. no 94/247 dated 12 October 1994, for £21,000 being the 1994 audit fee. No cash has been received from this client since August 1993.

2.   Tully Industries Ltd (partner TC)
I noted from the correspondence file relating to this client that in 1994 it carried out work installing double glazing at TC's house. Comparison of the

rates quoted in the correspondence with the data on the audit file suggests that the work was done at a discount of about 10 per cent – £350.

3. James Verity Ltd (partner BL)
Mrs Barnes's husband became a director of this company in 1994 and according to the 1994 accounts now owns 12 per cent of the share capital.

4. Hedon Holdings Ltd (partner SB)
Daniel Evans resigned from his post as audit manager with this firm in February this year to take up the job of financial accountant at Hedon Holdings.

5. Pembroke plc (partner JF)
In 1994, we billed this, our largest client, as follows,

	£
Audit of 1994 accounts	*39,000*
Taxation advice re 1994	*6,000*
Advice and assistance with installation of new computerized accounting system	*12,000*
Assistance with recruitment of new finance director	*1,500*
TOTAL	*58,500*

You will appreciate my concern about the size of the fees charged in relation to our total fee income.

I hope that this summary is helpful, and that we can now discuss the steps that need to be taken in advance of the JMU visit.

Regards

Mike

20.2 Memorandum from James Finch to Mike Dunn

Mike

Thanks for your memo and for the hard work you have obviously put in to this exercise. I do appreciate it, but I think there is a need to balance your comments with the commercial facts of the situation. Perhaps my comments below will help to clarify matters:

1. Bladon Ltd
I am well aware that this client has been experiencing cash flow problems for some time, but we are able to monitor the situation closely, given that we are preparing Bladon's quarterly accounts for submission to the bank. Glen attends all meetings of the directors to report on the company's financial situation, and he is confident that it will be able to trade out of its difficulties, provided that the bank's support is continued. On that basis, I am sure that we will be able to recover the outstanding fees.

2.   Tully Industries Ltd
Well spotted – but I don't really think you could describe the discount given as material in relation to the income of this firm!

3.   James Verity Ltd
I fully appreciate that this is a delicate situation. That is why I suggested that Sally should be replaced by Bill as engagement partner with effect from this year.

4.   Hedon Holdings Ltd
Obviously it was a blow to us to lose Dan, especially at such short notice. He was a highly competent employee, and had been the mainstay of the Hedon audit for several years, but our loss is clearly their gain, and I am sure that it is to our advantage to have a senior member of Hedon's staff who has such a close understanding of our requirements and procedures as auditors.

5.   Pembroke plc
On a personal note I have to say I'd be very sorry to lose this client, having been associated with it since I started my training with this firm in 1970! Fortunately, I don't think that will be necessary. The Institute guidelines state that fees for audit and other recurring work should not exceed 10 per cent of gross practice income. We fall within those limits. The other assignments we carried out for them last year – getting the new accounting system up and running and finding them an F.D. – were both one-offs, and hence don't fall into the calculation.

Please don't think I'm trying to fob you off. Issues like these are bound to crop up from time to time, and I'm sure it's a valuable exercise to sit back occasionally and make sure we haven't done anything that might compromise our independence.

James

QUESTIONS FOR DISCUSSION

1. Comment on James's responses to each of Mike's points. Do you consider them to be adequate? If not, what further action needs to be taken?
2. Are there any other issues not identified by Mike which the firm needs to consider?

Relevant reading

Institute of Chartered Accountants in England and Wales (1995), *Members Handbook*, 1.201 'Integrity, Objectivity and Independence', ICAEW, London

Case 21
Kemico Limited

BACKGROUND

Kemico Ltd manufactures a variety of chemicals which it supplies in bulk to industrial customers. Its factory at Gritborough employs 50 people, and its annual turnover in 1995 was £7.5M. During 1995, Kemico began to manufacture a new product, Zappo, for Immense Stores Ltd. Zappo's main ingredient is Zappolene, a toxic solvent. Quill & Co., Kemico's auditors, are currently completing the audit for the year ended 31 December 1995.

PEOPLE INVOLVED

Quill & Co.
Jason Smith: Audit senior.
Karen Lee: Audit partner.

Kemico Ltd:
Frank White, Production Manager.
Tom King, Managing Director.

DOCUMENTS

21.1   Quill & Co – Extract from 1995 audit planning memorandum

Laws and regulations affecting Kemico Ltd

Kemico Ltd is subject to the 1990 Environmental Protection Act (EPA). It is classified as a Part B business in the terminology of the EPA, which means that it is required to obtain local authority approval for its potentially polluting processes. The company is also under a duty of care to ensure that its waste products are safely and legally disposed of. In particular, records must be maintained of waste produced and disposed of. Waste must only be disposed of on a licensed site. If a subcontractor takes away the waste, it is still the company's responsibility to ensure that a licensed site is used. Our audit should include a check on the company's records and procedures to ensure that they are complying with the relevant environmental legislation.

21.2   Quill & Co – Extract from 1995 audit working papers

Compliance with environmental legislation

1.   *Local authority licence* – I reviewed the company's files and ensured that they had an up-to-date local authority licence for their emissions.

2. *Waste disposal arrangements* – for a sample of six solid or liquid waste products disposed of by the company, I reviewed the company's records to ensure that

- movements of these wastes appeared to be regularly recorded, with sequential control over movement notes;
- details of the subcontractor performing each disposal had been kept;
- details of the site to which waste was taken were available.

See the attached schedule for details.

For five of the six wastes sampled, all details were available, and as in previous years, procedures appeared to have been performed satisfactorily. For the sixth type, Zappolene residues, I could find no record of any disposal being carried out. This is surprising because there is no waste Zappolene stored on the premises.

Further work to be performed – discuss with works manager the procedures for disposal of Zappolene.

Jason Smith
31.1.96

21.3   Memo from Jason Smith to Karen Lee

I have just been to see Mr White to ask him why there were no records of any disposals of Zappolene this year. He was obviously reluctant to give me any information, but did say that there were special procedures in force with respect to Zappolene which had been drawn up by Mr King. Do you want me to speak to Mr King?

21.4   Memo from Karen Lee to Jason Smith

Jason – It's OK; this is obviously sensitive. I'll discuss it with Mr King when we have our usual end-of-audit meeting.

21.5   File note by Karen Lee

Note of a meeting with Tom King 5.2.96 (extract)

Waste disposal arrangements
I asked TK about the company's arrangements for disposing of Zappolene waste, as these seemed to differ from its normal waste disposal procedures. TK initially expressed surprise that I was querying what he described as a 'detail'. When I persisted, he said that there were 'difficulties' associated with Zappolene which the company had not anticipated when it started production of Zappo. To summarize a fairly lengthy explanation in non-technical language, the major difficulty is that the company has discovered that Zappolene residue requires to be specially neutralized before it can be disposed of by the

means normally used by Kemico. The treatment would mean that Kemico would have to spend £175,000 immediately on equipment and the recurring expenses associated with treatment would increase the production cost per drum of Zappo by 35 per cent. Kemico has contracted to supply Zappo to Immense Stores Ltd at a fixed price for the 3 years ending December 1997. Implementation of the treatment process would mean that Kemico made a loss of £150,000 annually over the 3 years of the contract. (Profit per the draft financial accounts for 1995 is currently £100,000).

Kemico is currently storing Zappolene residue in galvanized steel drums. These are dumped close to the perimeter of the Kemico site. TK stated that this was a temporary expedient, as the land immediately adjoining the dump is currently under development as a housing estate, and the drums will have to be moved to a different storage site. He agreed that the situation was in some respects unsatisfactory, but assured me that the company could see no viable alternative, given the disastrous financial implications of carrying out neutralization. The company has reviewed its tendering procedures to ensure that all relevant technical information is incorporated into future product costing, and production of Zappo will be discontinued as soon as the contract with Immense expires in 1997.

21.6 Facsimile message from Tony Cheung, Quill Management Consultants, to Karen Lee

Karen

Thanks for your fax. Why are you so interested in disposing of Zappolene? Anyway, for your information, it is highly toxic, and has been shown to cause nerve damage and birth deformities in rats. The only safe way of dealing with it is by neutralization of the residue. There was a case in the USA about 5 years ago where drums of Zappolene were dumped on a disused factory site. They broke down and the leakage seeped into the water table; the clean-up costs ran into millions of dollars. Let me know if you want any more details.

Best wishes

Tony

QUESTIONS FOR DISCUSSION

1. What issues are raised for the audit partner by the situation outlined above?
2. What action do you think she should take, and why?

Relevant reading

APB SAS 120: *Consideration of law and regulations*

Case 22
Playful Limited

BACKGROUND

Playful Ltd manufactures children's toys. It prides itself on being an innovative company, regularly developing new products. At the end of 19X8, it has 30 different lines in stock. Green & Co., Playful's auditors, are currently planning the audit approach for the year ending 30 September 19X8.

PEOPLE IN THE CASE

Green & Co.
Lucy Franks: Audit Senior.
Terry Dean: Audit Manager.

Playful Ltd
Frank Dobbs: Finance Director.

DOCUMENTS

22.1   Extracts from Green & Co's 19X8 audit planning memorandum for Playful Ltd

Results

Given below are estimated results for 19X8 (comparatives are 19X7 actual). Summarized balance sheets:

£000	19X8	19X7
Fixed assets	*2,700*	*2,315*
Current assets		
Stock	*2,175*	*1,880*
Debtors	*3,750*	*2,600*
Bank	*935*	*780*
	6,860	*5,260*
Current liabilities		
Creditors	*1,765*	*1,800*
Net assets	*7,795*	*5,775*
Represented by		
Share capital	*3,500*	*3,500*
Retained profit	*4,295*	*2,275*

Sales	5,600	5,300
Cost of sales	1,680	1,570
Gross margin	3,920	3,730
Expenses	1,900	1,850
Profit before tax and dividends	2,020	1,880

The company has had a successful year, with sales up by approximately 6 per cent. The composition of expenses is similar to last year: wages and salaries accounted for 45 per cent (19X7 43 per cent), depreciation for 22 per cent (19 per cent) and advertising and promotion 14 per cent (11 per cent). No other category exceeded 5 per cent of total expenses. Preliminary analytical review suggests that the financial results are in line with expectations.

Stock

Playful Ltd (P) is operating in a highly competitive and volatile market. Some toys become obsolete very rapidly as tastes change; others may become classics and enjoy steady sales for a long period. There is also the possibility that a new toy may be completely unsuccessful because of commercial mis-judgement. Stocks of toys for 19X7 (actual) and 19X8 (per draft balance sheet) are given below:

£000	19X8	19X7
Raw materials	375	350
Work in progress (WIP)	700	630
Finished goods	1,100	900
Total	2,175	1,880

This year's stocks include two major new lines, 'Bildit', a construction kit, and 'Fuzzies', a range of soft toys. Both went into production early in 19X8 and are being extensively promoted for the Christmas market. Stocks of 'Bildit' (finished goods, materials and WIP) total £300K and 'Fuzzies' £290K.

Sales and debtors

In previous years, P's major customers were large chains of department stores and toyshops. P has this year embarked on a new strategy of selling to smaller retailers, targeting independent toyshops and newsagents. This has had an impact on the size and age of debtor balances, as tabulated below:

Age in days	19X8	19X7
0–30	1,100	1,300
31–60	1,250	700
61–90	1,050	550

91 and over	*550*	*250*
Bad debt provision	*(200)*	*(200)*
Total	*3,750*	*2,600*

The number of customer accounts has increased substantially because of the new policy (from 130 to 300). The company's present computer system does not have sufficient capacity to deal with the increase in sales ledger accounts. A new computer system is to be installed early in 19X9. In the meantime, small customer accounts are being maintained on a manual system operated by a clerk recruited specially for the purpose.

Accounting systems

With the exception of the temporary manual system for debtors, there have been no changes to the company's accounting systems since last year. Our audit tests last year indicated a strong control environment with no serious weaknesses.

Audit approach

The audit approach will be based on an assessment of audit risk. This will enable an efficient and effective use of audit resources, by identifying those areas which present the greatest risk of misstatement and concentrating audit testing on them. This year, the areas which require particular attention appear to be debtors and stock (. . .)

Lucy Franks
1 September 19X8

22.2   Letter from Frank Dobbs, Playful Ltd, to Terry Dean, Green & Co.

Dear Terry

Normally I don't bother you about the way you run your audit – we've always been happy to leave things to you – but I'm rather concerned about the approach that Ms Franks is taking. Not that she isn't perfectly professional and so on – no problems there – but . . . she told me yesterday that the audit this year would be 'risk-based', i.e. that the auditors would identify those areas which they considered particularly risky, and concentrate testing on them. For us, she said that these were stock and debtors, and she explained that the team would be looking at them in considerable detail. When I pointed out that this sounded expensive, and that the quote for this year's audit hadn't sounded much higher than last year, she said that the additional work on stocks and debtors would be balanced by a lower level of testing on other areas which were judged to be 'low risk'. She quoted payroll as an example of this. Apparently the system was considered sound last year, and the payroll expense this time is consistent with expectations, so she doesn't think much needs to be done in the way of detailed checking.

Now I can see the sense of what Ms Franks is saying, but I have to say that I can see some serious drawbacks to her approach. Firstly, what does she mean by saying that an aspect of the accounts is 'high' or 'low' risk? This seems to me a matter of subjective judgement, which will vary from one auditor to another; and in any case, 'low' or 'high' in relation to what? What is the 'normal' level of risk?

Secondly, if 'risky' areas are those which are new or which involve a lot of subjective judgement, in any well-run company, they will already be getting attention by management, and intensive audit investigation may be unnecessary. I am concerned that the risk-based approach involves the assumption that 'no change' means 'no risk'. Ms Franks told me that payroll was taken to be low risk because the amount of the payroll charge was consistent with last year. If – heaven forbid – there had been a systematic payroll fraud over the last few years, the payroll charge might still look consistent, provided that the fraudster was careful.

I suppose that you will refer me to the concept of materiality – that your audit procedures are supposed to ensure that the financial statements are materially correct, with materiality designed as some percentage of turnover or profit. I can understand the concept, and its relevance to the people who read our financial statements, but I have to say that we need to be sure that the accounting systems are operating at a much higher level of accuracy. The knowledge that auditors are working to a materiality level of tens of thousands of pounds does little to deter a member of staff who is pocketing small amounts of petty cash – but small frauds (and errors) also cost us money and are bad for morale.

What I am saying, in short, is that I think a risk-based approach, although it is probably money-saving, actually offers less audit assurance, and is less useful to us as clients, than a more comprehensive approach that aims to give attention to all accounts areas, 'risky' or not. I'd appreciate your comments.

Best wishes

Frank

QUESTIONS FOR DISCUSSION

1. Explain what features of Playful's debtors and stock in 19X8 make them particularly risky. Suggest what audit tests Green & Co. might perform in order to address those risks.
2. Frank's letter is a criticism of risk-based auditing. How far are his criticisms justified?

Relevant reading

SAS 220: *Materiality and the audit*
SAS 300: *Accounting and internal control systems and audit risk assessments*
SAS 430: *Audit sampling*

Bibliography

Accounting Standards Committee (1995) *Accounting Standards 1995*, The Institute of Chartered Accountants in England & Wales, London.

Cadbury Committee (1992) *Report of the Committee on the Financial Aspects of Corporate Governance*, Gee & Co, London.

Easton, G. (1982) *Learning from Case Studies*, Prentice-Hall International, London.

Elkington, J. (1990) *The Environmental Audit*, SustainAbility, London.

Gray, R., Bebbington, J. and Walters, D. (1993) *Accounting for the Environment*, ACCA/Paul Chapman Publishing, London.

Gwilliam, D. (1988) Does care extend beyond the contract?, *Accountancy*, May pp. 17–18.

Hatherley, D. J. (1980) *The Audit Evidence Process*, Anderson Keenan, London.

ICAEW (1995) *Auditing and Reporting 1995/6*, The Institute of Chartered Accountants in England & Wales, London.

ICAEW (1995) *Guide to Professional Ethics*, The Institute of Chartered Accountants in England & Wales, London.

International Chamber of Commerce (1991) *An ICC Guide to Effective Environmental Auditing*, ICC Publishing SA, Paris.

Mills, C. (1990) *The Caparo Decision*, Coopers & Lybrand Deloitte, London.

Owen, D. (1992) *Green Reporting: Accountancy and the challenge of the nineties*, Chapman & Hall, London.

Pearse, C. (1994) Love thy Neighbour? *Accountancy*, November pp. 160–1.

Sherer, M. and Kent, D. (1983) *Auditing and Accountability*, Paul Chapman Publishing, London.

Wheatley, M. (1993) *Green Business*, Institute of Management/Pitman Publishing, London.